Dearest Joe,
    It's been a great
trip with you so far through
our lives together — I hope
the rest will be the best ever

Happy 60th!
            Love + kisses
                    Karin

FOOTPRINTS ACROSS

Oregon

FOOTPRINTS ACROSS
Oregon

BY MIKE THOELE

✖

GRAPHIC ARTS CENTER PUBLISHING COMPANY
Portland, Oregon

International Standard Book Number 1-55868-017-9 (Hardbound)

International Standard Book Number 1-55868-018-7 (Softbound)

Library of Congress Catalog Number 89-83847

Published by Graphic Arts Center Publishing Company

    P.O. Box 10306 • Portland, Oregon 97210 • 503/226-2402

© Guard Publishing Company

    P.O. Box 10188 • Eugene, Oregon 97440

Editor-in-Chief • Douglas A. Pfeiffer

Associate Editor • Jean Andrews

Designer • Carl Davaz

Cover Photograph • George Millener

Photography • Paul Carter, Carl Davaz, Pat Davison, Wayne Eastburn,

    George Millener, Andy Nelson, Rosanne Olson, Chris Pietsch,

    Dan Root, and Joe Wilkins III

Song Lyrics Page 15 © 1987, Goldline Music

    (Administered by Copyright Management, Inc.)

Typographer • Harrison Typesetting, Inc.

Printer • Dynagraphics, Inc.

Bindery • Lincoln & Allen

Printed in the United States of America

To Sandy,
who listens with patience
to tales brought home from the road

CONTENTS

SECTION III
FAST DOGS AND
WHIMSICAL LADIES

SECTION IV
LONELY GRAVES AND
DESERT CAFES

FOREWORD

ONE WAY TO KNOW OREGON is to know the land, another is to know the people. Mike Thoele has it both ways. He sees the land through the men and women about whom he writes, perceives it not only in its spectacular vistas of mountain ranges and jagged peaks, the sparse plains of the Great Basin, the blue-green of the western forests and emerald green of the valleys, the cascading streams, the ocean's surf pounding at the rocky shore, belying the name Pacific. All that he sees, but not in panoramic view or great murals.

With his subject as his camera lens, he captures the scene: dinner at Burns Junction, in the only cafe within three thousand square miles, a truck roaring over the undulating plain, "its red and orange clearance lights rising and falling in the distance like the portholes of some outbound ship," he searches for the site of a monument marking the spot in the Coast Range where a plane crashed during World War II, carrying to their deaths eight young American servicemen. He talks to the son of the woodsman who found the plane and to the contractor who built the monument. And he visits the site, an isolated wilderness above the Chetco River. The aluminum fragments, on that rare day of clear skies, gleam "brightly in the spring sunlight. Wild iris and manzanita finger their way through the torn metal. A dogwood tree bends gently forward—a leafy sheltering hand over the gravesite." The men remember, the son of the woodsman and the contractor, the struggle down the steep grade with equipment and building materials, the contractor rubbing the fresh cement by hand to make it smooth. On another spring afternoon in the Willamette Valley, Thoele talks with a man whose most persistent habit is laughing out loud. Who could regret that, he asks, "when the sun is laying its light on greening fields like new paint on a park bench and the aroma of cottonwood buds rises fresh from the riverside?"

But it is not so much what Thoele's subjects see that interests him as what they experience of the land, how it shapes their vision, challenges their strength or purpose, nurtures them in its congenial atmosphere. A ranch kid from eastern Oregon blows his chance at college, enlists for the Vietnam War, returns home with his arm shattered, but determined to go back to Asia as a helper, not a warrior. Unable to forget the ranch and the great vistas of eastern Oregon, he enrolls in land management at Oregon State, earns his master's degree, and goes into the cattle business for himself. Back at Oregon State, he completes his doctorate while his family holds on to the ranch. And then comes the chance to go to China, to the steppes of Mongolia, as an expert on rangeland management, his two visions now merged—help for Asia and preservation of the land he loves, whether it is Oregon or Mongolia.

One could go on: an eastern boy, taking his doctorate in biochemistry, teaching in college with increasing dissatisfaction, migrating to Oregon, finding congenial friends and congenial land, settling at last as a gardener with a vision, a dream of preserving species of plants that may become vital to the world's food supply, ancestral varieties with extremely high resistance to diseases, pests, and environmental change. Or a widow in the desert—proprietor of a lonely cafe and gas station; hostess to hungry cowboys, truckers, ranch wives, tourists; benefactor to those who are stranded, out of gas, or with flat tire or stalled engine; good Samaritan to accident victims—her spirit exalted by the land.

Or a young forester trained in an eastern university, employed by the Forest Service, manager for a private lumber firm, intent on keeping the logs rolling to the mills. The beauty of the forest gets to him. He draws the line, leads the fight to preserve a wilderness. Or a fly fisherman, reared on the flatlands of Kansas, with eight grades of schooling, a laborer, he drifts into Oregon, is entranced by the trout in the sparkling streams. He begins to experiment with tying his own flies. That leads him to the study of the insects that attract the trout, not the appearance only but to the feel of them, the hardness or softness, the substance of them, and that to the study of books on entomology, the development of his craftsmanship, the writing of books, a national reputation. And as a byproduct, the discovery of history, philosophy, psychology, anthropology, geology . . . Or the crew on the Coast Range mountain above Mist, attacking the land, planting trees, living in tents, fighting the rain and the steep ridges, "slipping, sliding, cursing, bickering, laughing . . . packing their sodden tree bags, swinging their heavy hoedags into a spattering black mix of ash and mud." One of them pauses. "There's a lot of satisfaction doin' this," he says. "Don't tell anybody. We're supposed to hate it."

And so, for thirty-five tales. Some of the characters are shaped by the land, some cradled and nourished by it, some fight it, but always the people are the focus of Thoele's attention. The stories are brief, easy-flowing, engaging narratives, some dramatic, some amusing, a few heroic, a few poignant, like the sensitive and moving story of the Vietnam vets at the exhibit in Eugene of the replica wall of the Vietnam Veterans Memorial. And always at their center, the people who help to define Oregon—and the nation, too. It is a book for delightful, discursive reading, and one to come back to for other tales or the re-reading of familiar ones.

Robert D. Clark
President Emeritus
University of Oregon

This is Oregon as seen through its people—natives, transplants, passers-by, latecomers, even some dead men . . .

ACKNOWLEDGMENTS

THIS WORK IS THE RESULT of a series of collaborations between a journalist and his sources. Most obvious are those whose lives and pursuits are detailed here, the generous interviewees who so graciously provided the raw material for this book. But for every one of them, there are dozens less obvious, a chain of passing acquaintances, friends, readers, co-workers and subjects of other stories who keep my stock of ideas fresh. Interesting people know interesting people. And it sometimes seems that one simply passes me along to the next, so that I may reap what they tell.

This satisfying assignment of roaming Oregon in search of its unusual citizens and interesting crannies owes its existence to *The Register-Guard*, the daily newspaper operated so creatively for so many years by the Baker family of Eugene, Oregon. Former City Editor Kevin Miller helped hammer the roving reporter concept into workable form. Managing Editor Doug Bates made his own contributions to the concept's evolution, including the "Northwest Journal" logo that identifies the stories as they appear in the newspaper.

Carl Davaz, *The Register-Guard*'s graphics director and the veteran of another "newspaper book" project, guides the photographers whose work, along with his own, accompanies the stories. He is the designer of this volume. His advice and counsel were invaluable. And so were the contributions of his troops—Paul Carter, Pat Davison, Wayne Eastburn, George Millener, Andy Nelson, Rosanne Olson, Chris Pietsch, Dan Root, Joe Wilkins III—who brainstormed and barnstormed with me as we chased words and pictures across endless miles of Oregon.

Over the years, a small squad of editors from *The Register-Guard*'s various sections has honed, corrected, and polished Northwest Journal, and its writer, as needed. In that fashion, the stories in this book have benefitted, more than the reader will ever know, from the touch of Cynthia Anderson, Sally Cheriel, John Conrad, Jim Godbold, Lloyd Paseman, Dean Rea, Lance Robertson, and a legion of copy editors.

Jean Andrews, associate editor at Graphic Arts Center Publishing Company, was the patient shepherd who so skillfully pushed and pulled, as the situation demanded, to get this project to completion.

At times, the stretch from the immediacy of the daily newspaper to the permanence of the bound volume seemed long indeed. Those whose assistance, advice, and encouragement helped bridge the chasm included Rick Baker, Sue Boyd, Joe Clark, Tom Detzel, Al Gemmel, Dave Johnson, Bob Keefer, Carolyn Kortge, Ken Metzler, Paul Neville, Melissa Pearson, Sharon Portier, Barbara Price-Brenner, and Bill Sweet.

INTRODUCTION

I REMEMBER BEST a night on the desert. An October moon rising to gild the Owyhees. Coyotes yipping in the draws. Nighttime chill slipping beneath the retreating fingers of twilight to draw the day's heat out of earth and pavement.

But Dan Root and I were not out there in the gloaming. Root, one of the several talented photographers whose work has helped mine come alive, had packed away his cameras. My notebook was stashed. Not for us the road on this evening. Not just yet. We sat instead behind the locked doors of the Burns Junction Cafe, guests for dinner at this tiny oasis in the sagebrush.

And what a dinner it was for the heart of cattle country. Emerging from the kitchen of the only cafe in three thousand square miles was a fresh salmon feast of mammoth proportions and epicurean quality. Caught on the coast only a day before, the twenty-pounder had been packed to the wide open spaces by one of the cafe-motel-gas station's small crew. It was a special evening for a few desert friends. But not so special that they could not whisk out extra plates for a pair of trail-weary story hunters from the flatlands.

When I am asked to explain this thing that I am privileged to do for a living, I think most often of that night. Its crystalline sense of isolation and remoteness was oddly marbled with reminders of the rest of Oregon and of America — a dinner on the Oregon desert with fish from the coast and visitors from the Willamette Valley. Around our table were lives with pasts or presents tied to logging and lumbering and railroading and millwork and ranching, to name just a few. Natives and newcomers, pencil pushers and stock branders, hired hands and paycheck signers, we picked the bones and passed the biscuits. The World Series played *sotto voce* on the television at one end of the room, one American experience as backdrop to another. Occasionally, a truck swept by on the highway and rolled onward across the desert ridges, its red and orange clearance lights rising and falling in the distance like the portholes of some outbound ship.

The road, of course, is what connects it all for me. I travel Oregon. I see places. I meet people and share lives. And I write. For four years now, *The Register-Guard,* Eugene, Oregon's daily newspaper, has made it possible for me to do this wandering and chronicling. Friends and strangers alike tell me it is the best job in Oregon. They get no argument. Around the nation, a few other newspaper journalists do the same sort of thing, traveling back roads and side streets in search of the people and situations that would not otherwise reach print. The Statehouse and City Hall, the politico and the VIP we largely leave to others. The significance of insignificant lives, the details of unusual occupations, the delights of obscure places are our stock in trade.

John McCormick, a *Newsweek* editor who was once the newspaper roving reporter in Iowa, estimates perhaps forty American newspapers have put experienced writers on the road and told them to visit the places where, according to the conventional wisdom, nothing ever happens. McCormick says the newspapers have television's Charles Kuralt to thank for the idea. Certainly, few were willing to invest in such ventures until Kuralt acquired a national following. But the newspapers that have tried it have found ready audiences. I know a few of those roaming writers now: Dave Johnson in Lewiston, Idaho; Chuck Offenburger in Des Moines, Iowa; Jerry Bledsoe in Greensboro, North Carolina.

Perhaps we do journalism in the most literal sense, like those who journeyed in the nineteenth century and ended each day with pen in hand. We travel, we see, we write. Much of what we view seems ordinary at first glance, the sort of things that others might ignore. But in viewing any one of them, holding it so some hidden facet catches light, both writer and reader can be surprised.

Oregon is fertile ground for this work. Its native stock runs to men who go down to the sea in ships and up to the top of tall trees in climbing spurs, to women who command backwoods outposts of commerce and fight fires in the forest, to families that operate century-old ranches. Its vaunted, and threatened, liveability makes it home to a newer strain, the thousands who are here by clear, conscious choice, not by accident of birth or employment. I make a large portion of my living off of that group—the rural artists, intriguing retirees, aging hippies, cottage entrepreneurs, wistful visionaries, forgotten semi-celebrities, perennial transients and misbegotten seekers who, being able to live where they choose, choose Oregon. And, for good measure, there is the touch of those who come but do not stay—the Asian deckhands, African students, European hitchhikers.

Out of this pursuit, I have become fascinated with lives. I am even fascinated with that fascination, which seems universal. Each of us has one, wonders how best to use it, and harbors some innate curiosity about the way others use theirs. It is the only reason I can offer, not that any other should be required, for a daily newspaper to find space and readers for stories about people who are of interest only because they live among us. I craft these stories, three of them a week when it goes well, like some cobbler making shoes at a bench. It is for the reader to decide whether they are anything of import. But this I know. The raw material is priceless. And I should always remain awed that people give it to me for nothing.

Mike Thoele
Cheshire, Oregon

Perhaps it is an Oregon disease, this willing trade of mere achievement for something as elusive as quality of life.

SECTION I

HOEDAGS
AND
RHINESTONES

I don't follow rainbows, big dreams, brass rings
I've already captured mine
— STEVE EARLE

PARTLY, I TRY TO DEFINE the Oregon work ethic. I see it every week, in one new manifestation or another. Perhaps I am coming to understand. Certainly, I have learned to recognize the Oregon tradeoff. It is the treaty that so many, in all walks of life, sign with themselves when they commit to live here, where they want to live, rather than to go where trade or profession or the conventional measures of careerism might dictate. Some have described it as an Oregon weakness, this willingness to sacrifice achievement for quality of life, to trade countinghouse green for nature's green.

But it seems more than escapism. In so many of the men and women I meet, commitment to the quality of work seems to underlie the preoccupation with quality of life and place.

Indeed, understated intensity often is the common denominator. It is there in the cowboy who will travel half a world away from home to maintain his toehold on the range. It is there in thirty-five-year-old tree planters who swing their hoedag tools with verve, proud at lasting another season in what is clearly a young man's game. It is there, shimmering in the rhinestones and sequins of a trapeze artist who flies alone, winter and summer, in a mountain meadow. It is there in an elite squad of plywood workers who hit the mill each day like Olympians coming out of the starting blocks.

Having made the choice for geography, they will work harder and better — doing what they must do to stay in this place and, perhaps, proving to themselves and to others that this is not the dropout's existence. For them, and for Oregonians like them, work is inextricably entwined with place. They can imagine doing it nowhere else. It is all of a piece.

He is only one wrangler,
but his struggle to preserve
the stockman's traditional
way of life and work spans
two cultures and two continents.

Wallowa
Autumn

THE MONGOLIAN COWBOY

SOMEWHERE UP THERE, Genghis Khan must have smiled. The old warrior who conquered Asia and threatened Europe, whose fierce tribesmen once controlled all the turf from Moscow to Canton, might even have managed a chuckle at the unlikely scene that Dennis Sheehy played out in Inner Mongolia on that summer afternoon.

Perhaps only the limits of thirteenth-century geographic knowledge prevented Genghis from making a run at the Americas. But here, on Asia's windblown steppes, was this American wrangler facing off against the Mongolians—a rough-riding cowhand from one continent taking on his counterparts from another. Partly, it was like a fight in a corral, an Oregon cowboy versus an Asian cowboy— and another and another and another, a Mongol horde lining up to do battle.

But this was no fray of flying Stetsons and roundhouse punches. The costumes were the studded leather vests, rainbow skirts, and bright pantaloons of an ancient culture. And the ground rules were the traditional one-fall-and-you're-out wrestling formula that old Genghis himself had watched around the campfires of his army. And, my, but wasn't that cowboy eating a lot of dirt.

"There must have been a thousand people watching," Sheehy says. "They all came to see this foreigner wrestle. I had to take on this guy who was ranked number eight in the country. And then the guy who was number twenty-six. I was going down quick, just woosh, woosh, woosh. So then they gave me this fifty-year-old guy. Only he'd been a top wrestler in his day. He beat me, too." He sips coffee and laughs at himself. He is, as he tells the story in his Wallowa County living room, the consummate Eastern Oregon cowboy. Dusty and a bit weary from a roundup day in the saddle, softspoken and almost embarrassed at spending an evening talking about himself—but clearly enjoying his family listening, laughing at his expense, and spurring him on at the pauses.

There is more to Dennis Sheehy at forty-two than stirrup-worn boots and work-worn jeans and blue eyes set in range-weathered creases. This is the Baker

County ranch kid who blew his first chance at a college education. This is the Vietnam vet who came home from his war with an arm nearly shot off and a head full of wistful, hopeful ideas about going back to Asia as a helper, not a warrior. This is the second-chance student who, over a period of fifteen hardscrabble years, knocked off bachelor's degrees in Asian studies and Mandarin Chinese, and a master's and a doctorate in range management. And this is the working Oregon rancher who, for three years running, packed his expertise and his family off for six-month stints on the wind-scoured steppes of Inner Mongolia, one of the earth's most isolated regions.

Sheehy went as a range consultant to a problem-plagued grassland area in the autonomous Mongolian region of northern China. It is a place where, even in reopened China, foreign visitors seldom penetrate and many of the niceties of twentieth-century living are wanting. The herders Sheehy met and worked with in Mongolia are horsemen from a lineage of skill and ferocity. The Great Wall was an unsuccessful attempt to keep their warlike ancestors from plundering China. In the 1980s, as a not-always-beloved ethnic minority within the Chinese population, most of the Mongolians stand only a generation or two removed from nomadism. The ones Sheehy went to serve were approximately as receptive to an outside expert as any group of prideful American cowhands would be.

"This was not a case of going to help some Stone Age people," he says. "These are people who have their own ideas. The local officials didn't know what to expect from me. Essentially, they'd had me shoved off on them by higher-ups. And they'd already had one consultant who only lasted a day and then left. I'm not sure what the herdsmen expected. I think most of them came to our first meetings because they wanted to see what a big-nosed foreign devil looked like."

The trek that had brought Sheehy — he was Shee-Hi to the Mongolians — to the isolated commune of Yihenoer was roundabout. At eighteen he had come off the family ranch at Durkee, in Baker County, and headed to Portland State University. He enjoyed the city, perhaps too much. He proved himself a good football player and a poor student. He dropped out of school in his freshman year, joined the Marines, and was posted to Vietnam. "I wasn't there long enough to get to know many Vietnamese personally," he says. "Mostly I had the negative kind of military experience. But I had always had this interest in Asia. And being there reinforced it." Four months into his tour a bullet shattered his upper right arm. He spent a night lying in a rice paddy, awaiting rescue and wondering if he would survive. For most of the ensuing year he underwent reconstructive surgery and therapy in a naval hospital in Bremerton, Washington. He mapped the cracks in the ceiling and thought about returning to Asia.

Dennis was discharged in 1968 and headed to the University of Oregon. Suddenly, the classroom terrain seemed less steep and decidedly more interesting. He rocketed through his double major in Asian studies and the Mandarin Chinese language in only three years. He met his future wife, Marcie Wyckoff, at the university and they were married before he graduated. Dennis took a fling at earning a master's degree in Asian studies, but gave it up. "The war in Vietnam was winding down and there didn't look to be much chance of getting back to southeast Asia," he says. "And the more I was away from the rural environment, the more I missed it."

So, instead, he headed off to Oregon State University, where he spent two years wrapping up his master's degree in range management. Then he took on a couple of years of state-funded game study work in the Steen Mountain region of southeastern Oregon. Although it never went away, the dream of returning to Asia was shelved. In 1976, Dennis and Marcie leased a ranch near Wallowa and went into the cattle business.

It went well enough at first. Their family grew to three children—Ryan, Carrie, and Cody. But by 1980, a recession was pinching Oregon's ranchers, and it pinched tightest on the new and undercapitalized ones. In 1981, Oregon State offered Sheehy a paid assistantship to conduct an elk study near Heppner. The money would be of help in keeping the ranch going. And the job, coupled with some classwork, would mean a doctoral degree. For three years, the family—with the help of relatives—kept the ranch afloat while alternating between living in Heppner, Corvallis, and Wallowa.

And then Asia surfaced again.

An old Oregon State contact told Sheehy that China was looking for an expert in rangeland management to work with the Mongolians. Population pressure, abandonment of the nomadic life-style, soaring animal populations, and overgrazing were threatening the grassland steppes. In February of 1985, after a twelve-hour train ride from Beijing and a day in a four-wheel drive rig, Sheehy got his first look at Yihenoer. He and the Chinese party officials and local Mongolian leaders felt each other out for a week. They were stunned when he announced that, if he took the job, he would bring his family. But they offered him the position.

For the ensuing three years, his family would spend their springs and summers on the steppes of Mongolia, living in cramped two room quarters, eating the local diet, and adapting to the limitations of a spartan culture. "We never thought about doing it any other way," Marcie says. "It seemed like an adventure and we definitely didn't want a long-term family separation. The kids were game. I was game. So we did it."

What you see is what you get with Dennis Sheehy. The academician is like the cowboy. When he speaks of the plight of the steppes, he does it with the same quiet, down-home style that he might use leaning over the hood of a pickup and assessing a ranch operation across the road. Except that this assessment is wide-angle. It opens with talk of global population pressures and a trend toward "desertification" as nomadic peoples settle into sedentary lives and begin using up the resources around them.

In Inner Mongolia, the nomadic life is all but gone. In broad outline, the plight of those who lived that life is a replay of the saga of much of the American West. "Sodbusters," Chinese farmers, move up from the south and fence off the choice rangelands. Government and population pressure reduce open range, discourage nomadic cattle driving, and inevitably compromise a way of life sacred to those who have followed it for generations.

"The biggest problem in Inner Mongolia is ecological degradation of the rangeland from overstocking," Sheehy says. "But the intrinsic problem is too many people. The Mongolians all have more animals than they should have. They have three cows to the acre on land that's a lot like northern Nevada. It should be thirty acres to the cow. Around the villages you have this ever-enlarging circle where everything is consumed and plants are killed out by overgrazing and trampling." Sheehy's search for solutions hit roadblocks at every turn. Some were laughable; all were frustrating. "The Chinese expected me to sit in my room and write grandiose management schemes about how to improve the rangeland," Sheehy says. "They said if I wanted to go someplace they would take me. They told me that there were these fierce dogs that would eat me and snakes that would bite me and bad men that would kill me. They wouldn't let me ride a horse because they were afraid I'd hurt myself. If they'd had their way I would have stayed in the administrative compound for three years. But I can't operate like that."

Sheehy's official mentors were given to long afternoon naps. So he began slipping away from the compound at Yihenoer. On foot and by bicycle, he ranged miles across the grasslands. The men and boys who herded the cattle, sheep, and goats became accustomed to seeing Shee-Hi, in his broad-brimmed cowboy hat, cruising the steppes. Slowly, cautiously, a dialogue began. The herders learned that the slow-talking foreigner was a man who would not hesitate to pitch in when there was a piece of work to be done with an animal. Out of sight of official watchdogs, Sheehy even got in some saddle time on the tough Mongolian cow ponies. It was a test, of sorts.

"They're real horsemen," Dennis says. "They really are. They're probably the equal or better than ninety percent of the American cowboys I've ever seen. They truly know horses."

But, as much as anything, wrestling became the cowboy's icebreaker. Sheehy learned early that the stylized Mongolian version of the sport was a cornerstone of male culture on the steppes. He saw that it was a judolike sport of speed and balance—no handholds permitted below the waist and a match ending when any part of a competitor's body other than the feet touches ground.

The inevitable day came when Sheehy was challenged by a herdsman. His opponent was an even match. The tussle ran fifteen minutes, long by Mongolian standards. It ended when both wrestlers tumbled ingloriously into a fresh manure pile—a story often retold to good effect in Yihenoer. The tale led to more wrestling challenges and to Sheehy's appearances in traditional Mongolian wrestling regalia at Yihenoer's summer festivals.

The grasslands were to prove a much tougher matter. Sheehy learned that the most obvious solution—reduction of herd size—was not a viable option. In the Mongolian culture, just as in the ranching country that Sheehy calls home, status is closely linked to animal ownership. So he turned instead to improving the food supply for Yihenoer's livestock. He persuaded some herdsmen to build fences, so that sections of pasture could be allowed to rejuvenate. To help animals withstand the long, hard Asian winters, he introduced fodder crops such as oats and corn.

Around him, the steppes where Gengis Khan's horses had pastured belly-deep in grass were a ticking ecological clock. Sheehy found vast sections of once-lush grassland with only a sparse cover of hardy native thyme—the last stage before desertification. "An ever-present feature of life in Inner Mongolia is the wind," he says. "It blows right out of Siberia with nothing to stop it. Some days the sky was filled with dirt. The land was trying to get up and walk away."

As Dennis learned, so did his family. "It got harder for the kids to go every year," Marcie says. "For the kids, there was not a lot of stimulation, not a lot of things to do, especially because our movement was so restricted. We finally got our bicycles in the third year. But I found the slow pace wonderful in many ways. I learned Chinese, so each year I made more friends. I had a lot of fun with my kids. We read a lot and played a lot of games, things that we Americans don't seem to do much anymore because we have so many gadgets to entertain ourselves. And every time, when I'd come home and get back into the fast-paced life, it was hard. I would hate to hear the phone ring."

Like others who have fought the uneasy, uncertain battles where culture and population pressure meet environment, Sheehy learned to settle for small successes. When the last of his six-month stints ended in 1987, he had seen a few Mongolians reduce herd sizes and accept the importance of pasture rotation and fodder crops.

He has returned to Yihenoer once since then and expects to be back in Inner Mongolia at least once more with a United Nations team that will evaluate the long-term effects of his work. Meanwhile, he struggles to maintain his own small ranch, aware of the irony that money earned keeping cowboys on the range in Inner Mongolia helps keep him close to an American life-style he has no desire to abandon.

"The problems over there aren't simple," he says. "There are social and economic factors the Mongolians will have to address in the long run. But I like to think that maybe I've planted a seed that will become something."

Epilogue: Dennis Sheehy spent the spring of 1989 in northeastern China and Inner Mongolia, working with other specialists to design a multi-faceted agricultural assistance project for the World Bank and the Food and Agriculture Organization of the United Nations. At the same time, he was under consideration for faculty positions at several U. S. universities.

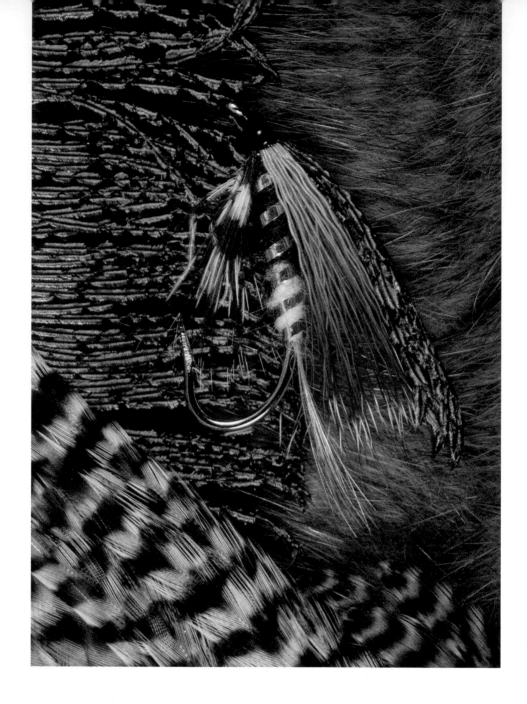

Polly Rosborough has brought
a scientist's precision, a fisherman's zeal,
and a craftsman's skill
to his curious art.

Chiloquin
Spring

THE BUILDER OF BETTER BUGS

MOST ASSUREDLY, it is in the hands. The eighty-four-year-old hands that flit, with deft confidence, about the tiny vise clamped to the scarred rolltop desk. Hands that move with surgeon's precision to whip together the tiniest snippets of fur and feather and hair and yarn. Big hands that still can make a younger man's knuckle cartilage pop and crack when Polly Rosborough delivers a handshake.

It is not exactly eye of newt and toe of frog, this strange science that Rosborough practices with pelts and plumage and dyes and lacquers in the hopelessly cluttered workroom at his Chiloquin home. Still, comparisons with witchcraft may not be entirely amiss—only a few hundred years ago an English gentleman suggested that, once the best possible fly had been tied, its effectiveness might be enhanced with the application of some powdered human skull or reduced cadaver fat. But, in truth, Polly Rosborough's art is more a biological alchemy, the turning of fur and feathers into insects so mouth-watering that even the cagiest trout in the toughest stream will lay down his life just for a bite.

"When I first came West and heard about fly-fishing and trout, I thought it was just for the smart guys," Rosborough says. "After a few years, I found out some of the smart guys were more stupid than I was. Most of the old-timers tried to do exact imitations of the nymph stage of insects that they saw. They'd make these hard little bodies with lacquer finishes. What I learned was that the natural nymph surface isn't hard and shiny, even though it looks that way to the naked eye.

"But if you put that nymph under a ten-power microscope, then you learn something. You learn that the surface is sort of rough or hairy, kind of velveteen. It flows and moves in the water. I learned that fuzzy nymphs catch fish. Imitating that fuzzy surface is more important than making an exact model of the nymph."

This is the world in which Polly Rosborough lives. In the process of becoming recognized as one of the nation's top flytiers, he has brought a scientist's precision, a fisherman's zeal and a craftsman's skill to the task of building better bugs. The flys he ties attract trout like pizza attracts teenagers. Since the time of the

---

Macedonians, nearly twenty centuries ago, this contest between the minds of men and the minds of fish has been waged. Back then, toga-clad anglers took note of the color of local flies, then tied red wool and rooster feathers to their bronze hooks. Over the ages, fishing, particularly fly-fishing, has acquired its own overlay of complexity, technology, and folklore—and not necessarily in that order.

For the non-fisherman, some primer-level information: Fish eat insects, mostly insects that hatch in or near water. Many of the insects go through transitional nymph stages en route to adulthood. Fish will bite on artificial flies constructed to resemble those nymphs, if the flies are used at appropriate times that correspond to the stage of the insect's natural development period.

Simple enough. But grown men and women can be driven to frustration trying to make the formula work.

Rosborough remembers that frustration, remembers thinking that he would never learn the ways of Wiley Trout. As a flatland farmboy, he had grown up hooking catfish in the lazy waters of Kansas and Oklahoma. With little more than an eighth-grade education, he had headed west and arrived in California. There he was introduced to fly-fishing. Entire generations of trout would come to rue that day. It took Rosborough a while to master even the initial complexities of the sport. But his interest never wavered. By the late 1920s, he was deeply involved in flytying. He worked to expand his knowledge of nature. He spent hours peering into the depths of water to watch live nymphs perform, minutely examined the stomach contents of trout he caught, and delved deeply into the textbooks of entomology, the science of insects.

He moved to the Chiloquin area in the late 1930s and came to call it home, although work often took him away. As he labored in the mills and shipyards of the West, his skill and reputation as a flytier grew. Finally, after a divorce in the early 1940s, he decided that he could support himself on tying and fur trapping.

He was correct. Through it all, the reading and the studying continued. His knowledge of the insect world moved into the realm of Latin scientific names, microscopes, and a fuller understanding of the entwined life cycles of insects and fish. "I never had much schooling," he says. "But I never let it keep me from getting an education. Right now, I'm about five million words into the Great Books of the Western World. I like history, things like Gibbon's *Decline and Fall of the Roman Empire*. I have a list of things I like. Psychology and philosophy, paleontology, archeology, anthropology, geology, zoology, biology, and aquatic entomology. That last one's the most important."

The self-educated man became the author of three fly-fishing books. His classic *Tying and Fishing the Fuzzy Nymphs* is headed into its fourth printing. His life's work is built around twenty-five western insects whose appearance, behavior, and life cycle he knows intimately. At his bench, he takes the materials of nature and of man—he uses some synthetic yarns these days—and spins them into fish catching-versions of the insects. The fur, feathers, hair, and yarn come from a variety of sources, incuding flytying supply houses, hunting and fishing friends, even the owners of a few golden retrievers and poodles.

His colorful flies, a few of them worn by women as decorative accessories, all have easily remembered marketing names. But almost every one of them is a representation of a specific stage in the development of a specific insect. The Black

From an old rolltop desk that is his laboratory and workbench, Polly Rosborough selects from treasures hidden in boxes and jars to recreate colorful insects of trout streams of America's West.

Midge is the *Chironomus larva,* the Great Western Leadwing is the *Isonychia velva,* the Golden Stonefly is the *Acroneuria californica.*

These days, Rosborough is recognized as an expert. He is cited as one of the country's top flytiers in Ernest Schwiebert's *Trout,* the two-volume bible of the sport. At eighty-four, Rosborough travels the West regularly, dispensing humor and irreverence in demonstrations at sport shows and fishing shops from Arizona to Washington. He has tied 750,000 flies in his life and is still good for a few dozen a day. At one point he had fifteen contract employees tying his designs. Currently, thousands of Rosborough-design flies, tied by women in India and Sri Lanka, are marketed by an Oregon company.

Rosborough has given up trapping, but only a couple of years ago he was still running a trap line and covering a half-dozen miles a day on snowshoes. "The hands are still steady," he says. "I can see some of the effects of age. Maybe for the first three flies each day they're a little shaky. And then they just get better and better each hour." The flytying, he thinks, can go on indefinitely. So can much of the travel. So Rosborough counts himself lucky. Someday, he knows, it will end. But even then, the fish will not have seen the last of him.

"Five guys here in Chiloquin have a copy of my will," he says. "They ain't gonna bury me. They're gonna burn me. And then those guys are gonna take my ashes up here to the mouth of Spring Creek. They'll take a bottle of whiskey along and they're all gonna take a shot. They're going to put the rest in an atomizer and spray it in the air so I'll get mine. Then they'll toss my ashes in the creek and I'll visit all those big fish I never caught."

Epilogue: The fish in Spring Creek will have to wait. Polly Rosborough rolled past his eighty-sixth birthday, still tying flies.

Winter and summer, she flies
swift and sure between sky and earth
in a lonely Oregon pasture,
with no certainty of what
she will ever do with her art.

Wimer
Autumn

THE EVANS CREEK FLIER

No CALLIOPE PLAYS. No canvas billows overhead. No ringmaster extols feats of derring-do. No drums roll. No rubbernecked audience, all Adam's apples and eye whites and babies on knees and fists in popcorn sacks, falls to silence and catches its breath as one. There is only the wind, cold now in November, and a hawk, gliding above and looking askance at an earthling imitator.

Planted in a pasture where Evans Creek flows out of the Cascade Range, the rig is all lines and pulleys and spars and nets, a vision as unlikely as a sailing ship moored in mid-Sahara. Up above, the improbable bird in this improbable bower soars back to the softest of landings on her mahogany perch. "This is easy and slow. In an act, everything is quick. You're never flatfooted. You're always styling. That's ninety percent of an act—presenting it. We'll come up here, I'll do a warmup swing and then it's boom-boom-boom, one trick after another. The act really lasts less than five minutes. The bar is swinging. All the time. It never stops."

Neither does Lisa Carlisle.

Two years have raced by since she last swooped beneath the big top, the star performer in the world's only all-girl flying act. And more than a decade has flown beneath her feet since the whole unlikely adventure began—joining the circus, performing across the length and breadth of North America, marrying the clown, feeling the tug of the eight-to-five world, leaving the traveling life behind.

There is a house now—a big rustic, rented place in the rolling hill country, out beyond the hamlet of Wimer, east of Grants Pass. Room for horses and dogs. Firewood to split and a garden to tend. And there is a radio job, the start of a career without greasepaint for her husband, Gene Carlisle. All the trappings and mappings of a workaday middle American life-style. And yet, the flier does not come easily to earth.

"It's still a part of my life. I can't imagine that I'll ever do without flying. Right now, I can't see a way that I'll perform again. Maybe I will. Maybe it will work out that way. I know I'm not going to sell my rigging. I'll always have it, even if it's just to play on by myself. I don't want to give it up. Sometimes I think maybe I ought to. But I know I won't."

So, at thirty, she works at her art, rehearsing with no opening date, her routine more certain than her future. She jogs ten miles and cranks out five hundred situps a day, pumps iron for hours, does dance workouts two nights a week. And she flies, through the hundred-degree heat of summer and the frosty days of winter, on an outdoor rig beneath the southern Oregon sky.

That is how it all began. She was nineteen then, up from California and visiting a sister. Down there, Lisa Carlisle had been a certifiable tomboy, playing football and baseball with the guys, doing long workouts and some competition with a running club. After high school graduation, she worked a bit in a gas station and on a street-striping crew.

And then, on her trip to Oregon, she saw the newspaper ad. "It said, 'Circus act needs girls. Must be free to travel.' That's all. I figured it might be working the concession stand. But it sounded like fun. A friend of mine wanted to check it out, so I went with her. We went out there, in the country outside of Grants Pass. There was this old man there. He told us about the all-girl act. And he had the rigging set up. I was just hooked. I took one look and said, 'I want to do that.'"

He was Del Graham, at sixty-four a circus veteran, a former trapeze performer, a one-time television actor. Years earlier, on a bet, he had organized the only all-girl flying act. "The Flying Viennas," he called them. He had been on the road with the act since then, touring with big circuses and appearing at major fairs. A few months before, he had fired all the troupe except catcher Patty Regis and moved his winter quarters to Oregon. Now, he was rebuilding.

Glamour may have been part of his past, but in 1975, as Lisa Carlisle stood in wonderment beneath the trapeze rig, earthiness was his stock in trade. At five-foot-two, stooped by injuries from his circus days, he was a profane little troll of a man. He had a patriarchal beard that drooped to mid-chest, a penchant for launching his day with three jiggers of bourbon in his coffee cup, and only a passing familiarity with soap and water. And he intended to recreate the Flying Viennas by teaching novices how to fly.

Many came but few stayed. Lisa Carlisle stuck it out, but her friend was among the first to depart. Another southern Oregon candidate, Maureen Fitzgerald, signed on for the dubious privilege of working outdoors in that Oregon winter of 1975-76, learning an arcane art from an aging performer who was long past being able to demonstrate it.

"It was so cold," Lisa recalls. "We wore thermals under our leotards. We'd sit by the fire as long as we could, then run out and climb the rigging. Now, when I teach someone, they can watch me and see how it's done. But all we had was a little old man standing on the ground, telling us to do this and do that. And he could be a mean old man. He'd stand down there and swear and throw rocks at us. There were times at practice when Maureen and I were so cold, but we wouldn't come down because we were scared. We'd stay up on the rigging because we knew he couldn't come up and get us."

"I can't imagine that I'll ever do without flying," Lisa Carlisle says of the endless hours of training. "I don't want to give it up. Sometimes, I think maybe I ought to. But I know I won't."

Eventually, it all came together. The reconstituted Flying Viennas—with the veteran catcher, the two southern Oregon rookies, and an experienced flier from Florida—were ready. Even though she was a new hand, a "First-of-May" in circus parlance, Lisa Carlisle was handling the toughest tricks in the group's routine. Graham's agent had no trouble booking the act into a string of good-sized circuses and big fairs.

They hit the road in Graham's bus. The former tomboy and gas pump jockey, already accommodated to false eyelashes, glued-on rhinestones and sequined costumes, began learning the vagaries of circus life. They had been scheduled to open with a circus in Oklahoma, but the show folded. Quick phone calls to the agent produced a new booking at a big indoor arena in southeastern Washington.

"My first show. It was Walla Walla or Yakima, I don't remember which. The bus broke down on the way. We showed up on the lot. Not very impressive—a flying act in a rental truck with two First-of-Mays. The crowd was huge. Maureen and I had never been in front of an audience before. It just sort of hit me. In school I was the kind of kid who got sick when I had to stand up and give a book report. I was so shy.

"And we were terrible that night. Patty was great as a catcher, but the other two girls blew all their tricks. I hit all of mine. Then I blew it on the ground. When you're done you're supposed to pop out of the net and walk over to the ring and style like a pro and take your bow. I just kind of walked out in a daze."

Soon enough, though, the Flying Viennas soared. For four years, they trekked the United States and Canada, sometimes playing entire seasons with the same circus, and at other times opting for spot dates at state and county fairs. There was a routine of sorts—March to November on the road, with the season always ending in Florida.

In those years, Lisa Carlisle's parents, who had all the classic reservations about a daughter running off to join the circus, got their first view of her flying above the arena. They loved it. It was during that time, too, that she and Gene Carlisle, the clown, met while pushing aside camels to get to the showers in the circus' winter quarters. Like her, Gene was a newcomer to circus. They were married in 1978 in her parents' Florida home.

"I liked being a flier. I liked my job as a performer. But I had mixed feelings about being on the road. It's a weird life. It's a very tight community. It's like a little neighborhood, where everybody has a niche that's based on the job they do. To some people who were born in the circus, it's all they know. For me, even though I loved the performing, one part of me wanted a stable home. I had horses back in Oregon. I missed them. It was that way for Gene, too. He liked clowning and he got to be a producing clown—sort of the boss clown. But he has a lot of other abilities and he didn't see himself staying in the circus forever."

Meanwhile, Del Graham's health was failing. Internal pressures were pulling the Flying Viennas apart. The act broke up in 1979. Gene and Lisa Carlisle came to Oregon. In 1980, Graham died at the age of seventy. Lisa grieved. "He was hard. He was a very hard old man. But he taught me to fly. He gave me that. I can't forget him for that."

For two years, the Carlisles lived a normal existence, with a home, regular hours, jobs, paychecks. But the circus was not so easy to leave behind. In 1982,

Lisa and Patty Regis bought a rig and began assembling a new act. They spent months in recruiting, training, and costuming, learning for themselves some of the difficulties that their old teacher had endured. When the time came to name the act, the choice was easy: "The del Grahams" went on the road.

Gene Carlisle traveled with them. Jobs weren't hard to get. They landed good bookings, including an appearance in a Canadian network television special. But Lisa Carlisle found that holding the act together was another matter. "It was amazing, but you couldn't find people who wanted to work. They wouldn't take their responsibilities as performers seriously. You'd hire girls, spend money for costumes and then they'd leave."

In the summer of 1983 the del Grahams folded.

Since then, the rig has stood in the pasture along Evans Creek Road, with horses grazing beneath it. Gene Carlisle pursues his job. And so, in her own fashion, does Lisa. Most of her daylight hours are devoted to conditioning and to working out on the rig in the limited fashion that is possible without a flying partner. Sometimes Gene stands on the narrow platform with her, assisting with setups and gently critiquing.

But, for her, it is training without a goal. The flier and the clown know they easily could return to the circus and pick up jobs in existing acts. But she wants him to have the opportunity to succeed in other things. And, for her, the attractions of horses in the pasture and life in the Evans Creek Valley compete all too favorably with the regimen of rhinestones and road life, even when Gene encourages her to consider putting together another act.

The ability to make split-second decisions in midair doesn't necessarily carry to ground level. "It's hard to think of not performing again. I want to. I'm real torn. I like having my horses with me. I like living a life where I come in the house and cook dinner. Being on the road is tough. But I imagine, someday, I'll perform again. I just can't say. I guess I don't know."

Epilogue: In 1987, the Carlisles took a last year-long fling at the performing life, with a non-touring animal-and-flying act based in Oregon. When it folded, they settled a few miles from the Evans Creek Valley. Now their lives are built on regular workaday jobs, home-buying plans, and deepening Oregon roots. And Lisa still flies.

I n the small and exclusive world
where the skills of close-quarter combat
and secret operations are respected,
the old warrior's name is a household word.

Scottsburg
Winter

THE THINKING MAN'S RAMBO

It is an arcane profession, this business of being recognized as one of the world's experts in stopping a mob, or operating behind enemy lines, or killing a man with knife or bare hands. An unlikely niche, too, for an Oregon country boy who marched out of the University of Oregon in the spring of 1939 with a degree in business administration.

But a war was brewing then. And, for Rex Applegate, it was a war that would lead him in unexpected directions and leave him with a set of skills that would shape his adult life. It happened to others, too. For some, World War II became a staging area for unexpected careers as reconstructive surgeons or airline pilots or rocket scientists.

Still, for the thirty-year-old lieutenant colonel mustering out at war's end as the Army Intelligence expert in some of the nastiest of the nasty business that goes on in war, another sort of peacetime career might have seemed in order. It would not play out that way.

"Someone always needed what I had," Applegate says. "I never expected it to turn out like that. But the war just put us in a time and place where I had unlimited resources and the opportunity to learn anything I wanted to know."

He walks to a shelf loaded with wartime mementos and pulls out a book entitled *Lock Picking and Safecracking.* "We had to spring a guy from Sing Sing to get this written. We found out that he knew more about it than anybody else, so we got him. That was the kind of thing we could do. And sometimes that was the kind of people we had to deal with."

Applegate is seventy-one now, four decades beyond the heady years when he helped train America's first espionage agents and commandos, served as a bodyguard to President Franklin Roosevelt, and schooled a generation of real-life American fighters in the kind of skills now glorified in Sylvester Stallone movies.

Sitting in the study of his Scottsburg home and watching the Umpqua River riffle past, he is a sort of thinking man's Rambo. The world — or at least that part of it that deals with the skills of warfare and clandestine action — still beats a path to his door. Small arms manufacturers from around the globe ship him new products for testing. Military historians and writers on combat practices come seeking his views. His books, with titles like *Kill or Get Killed* and *Riot Control: Materiel and Techniques,* continue to go through new printings. National law enforcement groups call on him regularly for speaking engagements.

Not exactly the circle to make an old soldier a household word. But in the specialized and sometimes secretive world where such skills command respect, Applegate's reputation is well-established. William Cassidy, a United States expert on political kidnapping, political assassinations and various forms of close-quarter combat, has described Applegate as a man who has contributed more than any other American to the development of pistol combat skills.

Cassidy sees Applegate's influence touching every branch of the American military and law enforcement establishments. "Rex Applegate must certainly be combat shooting's finest instructor," Cassidy wrote in *Quick or Dead,* a meticulous study of the history of pistol combat. "Indeed, if you have received any instruction in close-quarter combat shooting at any time since 1944, you were influenced by the work of Rex Applegate."

The beginnings of it all came in the months immediately before the bombing of Pearl Harbor. Applegate, a native of rural Yoncalla, Oregon and a descendant of the famed pioneer clan that has its name attached to pieces of history and geography all over the southern part of the state, was a newly minted Army lieutenant. He was assigned to a unit that was seeking evidence of Japanese espionage and offshore activity from Northern California to Mexico. Then came a cryptic telegram instructing the young lieutenant's commanding officer to send him immediately to the "Coordinator of Information" in Washington, D.C.

The coordinator was the legendary Colonel Bill Donovan. His operation would soon become the OSS — Office of Strategic Services — the United States government's espionage and intelligence branch, and the forerunner to the Central Intelligence Agency. Early in 1942, Applegate, who was part of the first handful of Army officers chosen for the OSS, stood before Donovan's desk, wondering about his future. Donovan quickly sketched his plans for a super-secret agency that would operate outside normal military channels and train Americans to work behind enemy lines. "Then he reached in his desk," Applegate recalls. "He pulled out $50,000 in cash and handed it to me."

The lieutenant's assignment was to go to a remote Forest Service camp near Thurmont, Maryland, and use the money to convert it to a training school for the OSS. The spectacularly beautiful site — it is now Camp David, the presidential retreat — offered a pleasant surprise. "It had been a Civilian Conservation Corps camp," Applegate says. "It had a lodge and barracks and blankets for the beds and a fully equipped mess hall. In no time at all, I was back telling Donovan the place was ready. He thought I was a pretty hot pistol. I never told him any different."

When Donovan began assembling the school's specialized faculty, Applegate was given the job of coordinating pistol, knife, and hand-to-hand combat instruction. It was a natural assignment for a six-foot-three-inch Oregon country boy who weighed 230 pounds and had acquired an Army reputation as a crack marksman and something of a barroom brawler. Donovan's projects had the highest federal priority. Applegate and the other officers had *carte blanche* to pull in any civilian or military expert they needed for their schooling operation. Some of those experts, such as famed British commando officers W. E. Fairbairn and William Sykes, came from across the Atlantic.

As Applegate assembled those experts and created his school of lethal arts, he became an instructor himself. He also subjected many of the deadly skills to rigid academic analysis, using photography to dissect the movements of skilled knife fighters and quick-shot pistol experts. The work became the foundation of the books he would write later.

As soon as Donovan's school began to function, Applegate and another OSS officer were sent to train with British commando and espionage forces. Applegate worked under Lord Louis Mountbatten and was one of a handful of agents put through a select British assassin's school. He is the school's only living graduate. During his time with the British forces, Applegate also participated in some reconnaissance missions with the commandos, crossing the English Channel and going into Fortress Europe long before the Allied invasion. "It's not the kind of thing you should talk a lot about," he says. "It was a chance to use some of the things I was teaching. But we got in and got out with no trouble. GI's in the trenches had it a lot tougher than I did on those missions."

Applegate was scheduled to accompany a commando raid against a German radar facility at Dieppe, France, in August 1942. But he developed a lung ailment. The unit he would have been with was wiped out.

Back in Maryland, Applegate's knowledge of assassination operations made him the bodyguard of choice after Roosevelt began using the OSS camp for a retreat. On one occasion, when British Prime Minister Winston Churchill made one of his secret flights to the United States, Applegate was the only person present for a series of angry debates between the two leaders. "I asked the Secret Service guys what I was supposed to do if Churchill hit him," Applegate recalls. "They told me to let 'em duke it out."

In 1943, Applegate, still honing his knife and pistol skills, moved from the OSS to a newly created Army intelligence branch which needed his expertise. He also was told that, because of his lung problem, he would never get a combat assignment. It was a disappointment, but he compensated by bringing out the first edition of *Kill or Get Killed* and by developing at Camp Ritchie, Maryland, a training operation that still is mentioned in military journals.

"The Camp Ritchie operation was another one of those deals where I was lucky enough to get whatever I needed," he says. "We had a fully equipped machine shop. We could build whatever we wanted. We created an entire German town, with all the buildings around a village square." Inside those buildings, ingenious pop-up targets and other shooting and knife attack tests challenged Applegate's students. On the grounds outside, his instructors — veterans fresh from the battle-fields and behind-the-lines operations of Europe and the Pacific — passed on their skills to new intelligence operatives.

Applegate also was the commander of two little-known military demonstration units. The groups, one "German" and one "Japanese," were actually composed of American GIs who used enemy equipment, uniforms, and tactics so that United States experts could analyze enemy operations. Applegate's Japanese unit was ethnically authentic: its troops were Japanese-Americans who had been rotated back to the States from combat units that had distinguished themselves in the European theater.

When the war ended, Applegate headed to Mexico. He spent most of the next twenty years there. Parts of that time are a closed book. "I kept up my contacts with people in our government," he says. "Some of what I did was private enterprise. I was doing some consulting and training, and selling military and riot control equipment to governments in Central and South America. But some of what I did is still classified information. I don't talk about it."

The Army frequently called him back as a consultant. He helped devise training programs and brought out revisions of his first book. During the fighting in Korea in the early 1950s, he was in that country as a civilian. There was some frustration in those years, too. As the Cold War and the Nuclear Age progressed, Applegate could see the American military establishment moving toward a high-technology view of warfare that ignored the sort of physical combat skills that were his specialty.

"Then the '60s came," he says. "We got into Vietnam and it wasn't World War III and it wasn't the kind of all-out electronic warfare that we'd been told the future was going to bring. It was jungle stuff at close quarters. And then we started having riots in the cities. Nobody was prepared for that, either."

In the mid-1960s, the Army summoned him from Central America. He spent the next decade revising training manuals and bringing out a reconnaissance manual, *Scouting and Patrolling*. In his south-of-the-border weapons work, he had become involved in equipment and training for mob situations. For a while, he added riot control information to new editions of *Kill or Get Killed*. In 1968, he brought out a separate book on riot control tactics.

The federal government moved him around the country to civil disturbances in those days. If campaign ribbons were awarded for domestic battles, he would be wearing ones from places like Watts, Detroit, Berkeley, and the 1968 Democratic National Convention in Chicago. To this day, Applegate remains angry about how American cities handled those conflicts. In his view, political interference always left the police in the position of being unable to act until situations deteriorated. "My first rule is to get the mayor out of the picture," he says.

In his riot-control book, Applegate advocates an early and strong display of strength by authorities. His views favoring the use, under some circumstances, of devices such as electric prods and chemical Mace would not play well in the ranks of civil libertarians. No regrets there for Applegate, whose conservative and authoritarian political views do not send him looking in that direction for support. But he does maintain that the use of such non-lethal devices is preferable to the measures that more trigger-happy experts espouse. His book, while it offers ample instruction in disabling and crippling techniques, emphasizes using the lowest possible level of force, working to achieve early dispersal of mobs and always leaving crowds an avenue of retreat.

For Applegate, the best situation is one in which no confrontation at all develops. Tom McCall, Oregon's governor during much of the Vietnam era, endured criticism for sponsoring a diversionary rock festival to head off the demonstrators at a 1970 American Legion convention. But Applegate, who was a consultant to Oregon officials during that tense summer, considered McCall's move an enlightened decision.

In the 1980s, Applegate feels that he once again is seeing the lessons of the recent past being forgotten. "My big concern now is that riot control is no longer on the police agenda," he says. "There's a lot of unrest, a lot of terrorism now. If we get into another round of mob disturbances in this country, we're not going to have the expertise to deal with it."

Occasionally, Applegate gets the chance to express those views as a speaker at conferences on terrorism, military tactics, or law enforcement. But there are other matters to occupy his time. Back in World War II, he and Fairbairn, the British commando hero, sketched out an improved design for a legendary combat knife that Fairbairn had created. The revision never got into production, and Fairbairn has since died. But in 1982, Applegate arranged for manufacture of the new Applegate-Fairbairn knife. It sells briskly and has become a weapon of personal choice for many men in special forces and commando units around the world.

In the late 1970s, Applegate built his retreat on the Umpqua, in an area that his pioneer ancestors explored and settled. He and his wife, Carole, share the riverside spot with three dogs and seven cats. He works every day at some facet of his field. Military publishers frequently send him manuscripts for review, and hardware manufacturers remain eager to get his evaluation of their products.

"I'll keep it up as long as anyone is interested in what I have to say," he says. "I plan to stay busy until it's time to go to that big combat range in the sky."

Epilogue: Since 1986, Lt. Col. Rex Applegate (Retired) has brought out yet another combat knife. He travels regularly to Washington, D.C., and continues work as a consultant for military and law enforcement organizations. He lectures frequently on Central American politics.

A priest without a flock,
he is content to work at making
the Christians of one world
understand the Christians of another.

Trail
Summer

FROM RUSSIA, WITH FAITH

In his priestly black robe and his flowing monastic veil, he is scholar, monk, historian . . . and comedian.

He is Father Andrei Urusov, he is seventy-three years old, and after five hours, he is still not finished weaving this ornate verbal tapestry of doctrine, history, mysticism, psychology, faith, and political science. On and on it goes. The warp and woof of it, this lecture and sermon and political speech, is his intricate analysis of the psychology of communist Russia and its leaders. But shuttling through it all is his concern for his beloved Russian Orthodox Church, once the cultural and social pillar of his nation before the communist revolution, now an oppressed shadow of its former self.

In his tiny home on the upper Rogue River, fifteen thousand books in a half-dozen languages are there as backdrop for his running dissertation. So, too, are seven decades of a variegated life that has been bounced about the globe by the Russian Revolution, two World Wars and his own penchant for travel and talk. On his table is a simple repast of cheese and tea. Beside it is the wooden bench where he sleeps each night without mattress or blanket. In the adjoining room is the icon-decorated chapel where, each morning, Father Andrei performs the ancient liturgy of the Orthodox rite.

But enough looking now. More talk. In a Russian accent as thick as borscht, Urusov marches off on a tangent, a wildly improbable story about being stopped by a policeman in San Francisco while driving a flower-painted Volkswagen borrowed from a "heepie." The story is longer than the Golden Gate Bridge. But in it the perplexed officer cannot decide whether he has found a stolen car or some strange variety of aging black-robed bohemian.

"Finally, cop does not know what to do with me. He does not know if I am thief or heepie, so he lets me go," says Father Andrei in mock wonderment. "Far out!" As the unclerical words pass his lips he whips his hand to his mouth, like an impish small boy who has let a profanity slip in front of his mother. That, too, is part of the act for this bearded, patriarchal man of God who has his own ways of softening up audiences that seem to be too reverent. In this small house, twenty-five miles upriver from Medford, he has studied and prayed for more than a decade, mixing hard work and quiet contemplation with a ready humor and numerous far-ranging lecture tours.

Among America's three Orthodox churches that claim Russian roots, Father Andrei Urusov is known as something of a lone ranger, an educated and colorful man who bounced into this country after World War II. A renegade perhaps, but a benign one. He has been supporting himself by his wits, lecturing and teaching – some would say entertaining – ever since.

"He has a fascinating background," says Clarence Rippel, the academic dean of Lincoln University in San Francisco, where Urusov taught in the 1960s. "If the Russian Revolution hadn't come along, he would have been a prince. He has a certain imperious air about him, but with a lot of humor. Students loved him. There were times when he was traveling 200,000 miles a year with his lecturing, driving all over the country in an old Mercedes. One of the radio talk shows on KCBS here had him on all the time. He was a big hit."

Father Andrei and those who have known him over the years tell the story of a son born to a Russian noble family in the twilight of the Czarist age, then orphaned in the Russian Revolution of 1917-1920. He was spirited out of Russia by relatives and raised by Russian expatriates in Belgium. As a young man, he was attending college and preparing to enter the priesthood when World War II erupted. He spent most of the war years in Italy as a seminarian. At the age of thirty, just after the war, he was ordained by a Russian bishop in Rome.

"After the war, I want to study," he says. "So I went to Ireland. It was the only nation that would give visa to a Russian refugee. I learned English there. I tell people my accent is Irish."

By 1948, he was in Shanghai, teaching in a colony of forty thousand Russians and Poles who had retreated there during Russia's political unrest of the previous three decades. Peace was not to be their lot. As the nationalist forces of Chiang Kai-shek retreated and the communists under Mao Tse-tung advanced, Urusov fled with six thousand of the Russians and Poles to a small island refuge provided by the Philippine government. Tuberculosis caught him there. He nearly died, but American Catholic missionaries rescued him, hospitalized him in Manila and arranged his transportation to Southern California in 1950.

Though he had traveled far, he was an unworldly man who had been sheltered for years by the seminary and the close-knit Russian refugee community. Every new Americanism he heard, he took literally. "I get off the boat and I am hungry. The people who meet me ask if I would like to go to drive-in restaurant and have hot dog," he says, his face replaying the puzzlement of a moment nearly forty years ago. "I say, 'I will try.'"

Soon he was at Fordham University in New York, helping establish a Russian studies program. Then came the University of Montreal, a period of study in Europe, and completion of a political science doctorate that was a far-reaching, multidisciplinary analysis of the psychology of communist Russia and communist leaders. By 1960, he was back in San Francisco, where he established a small non-profit institute with a library of works on communism, Russian history, and the

Father Andrei Urusov's life beside the Rogue River at Trail is largely an existence of prayer, contemplation and reading, broken by occasional forays on the lecture circuit. Though he has no congregation, neighbors from the remote region around his rural home occasionally come to share with him the celebration of the Orthodox Mass in the icon-filled chapel he has created.

FROM RUSSIA, WITH FAITH

Russian Orthodox church. He used that as a base for lecture engagements that took him all over the United States, speaking to campus, church, and civic groups.

"I work to explain the power of communism through psychology and philosophy and history and sociology and geography and political history," he says. "But especially the psychology. You take the communist leaders and analyze their pattern and make a conclusion. I see their training is psychologically and morally deep enough to compare it to the training of priests. For them, it is a profession. They are like a religious order. Like monks. But they have a mentality that makes them ruthless. Even Gorbachev. I do not think he is anything new."

His work has other facets. Much of his lecturing has been in fulfillment of a self-appointed mission to explain Christian Russia to Christian America. Others took up that same mission in 1988, the anniversary of a thousand years of Christianity in Russia. But for Father Andrei, bringing to Americans an understanding of the rich history and tradition of the Russian Orthodox Church has been a project of thirty-five years. "I earn my living from teaching like that," he says. "It is not much. I do not go around shaking pockets. But sometimes people give me a little and I survive."

His view of communism and the pressures it has brought to bear on the church in Russia is long and complex, a pendulum that swings from scholarly analysis to philosophizing to anecdotes from five visits to Russia in recent years. And all of it is laced with humor. His style — animated expressions, precise timing and a studied air of puzzlement at being the foreigner in a wondrous new land — is much like that of Yakov Smirnoff, the expatriate Russian comedian who has been well received in America. Father Andrei will roll out the act anywhere, on schedule in a lecture hall or impromptu at a roadside cafe.

"Always I want to know, what is the history and the ancestry of the people I talk to," he says. "Makes much difference in how they listen. Americans are like teenagers: they cannot listen for longer than forty-five minutes. The German or the Dutchman, you tell him a joke today and he laughs tomorrow. Italians and Russians, when they gather at dinner, all talk at the same time. Is a blessing. If they listen they would disagree.

"Once I talk in Alabama. To Baptists. Very stiff and no laughing. They do not know what to think of me. So I ask them if they know what is under my robe. All of a sudden they are listening. They are afraid I will show them. I tell them, is only 220 pounds of humility."

Father Andrei came to Oregon in the late 1970s, to live at Trail in the small house provided by a California benefactor. He earns his keep by working on the land around the house and by seeing that the place is painted and maintained. Inside, the home is crammed with books. They fill every room and overflow onto the tables and window sills. His bed is nothing more than the narrow, wobbly bench for a table that sits in his study. "In ten years, we fall only three times, the bench and me," he says. "Before sleep, I make up my mind not to fall down. I just lay down. Every night before I go to sleep I try to say three Hail Marys. I always fall asleep before first one is finished."

Two rooms of the home have been converted to a small Orthodox chapel, with veiled sanctuary, candles, and exquisite icons. Often, as Father Andrei performs the morning liturgy of the Orthodox rite there, he is joined by worshippers, residents of the rural valley who have come to know him over the years. A few he has baptized.

He still travels a bit. Among adventures he likes to recount were two unannounced visits to the Soviet consulate in San Francisco, where he bearded the communist lion in its den and cadged Russian magazines and Communist party literature from officials there.

"The first time I went there I walk into the middle of a big reception," he says. "They are surprised to see me, a Russian priest, in the consulate. I am easy to see. So I say, 'Well, I'm here. Anybody want any confessions? Spiritual advice? Here I am.' They don't know what to do."

For Father Andrei, the work seems more important than its effects. Numbers, dates, dollars, and the conventional milestones of society interest him little. As a priest, he has no flock, counts no sheep. These days he gets fewer lecture dates, and he is in arrears on his major financial responsibility, the property taxes on the house. He worries only a little. His faith, though, is a serious matter. And so is his elaborately defined view of communism's workings. But within the 220 pounds of humility is a man who can look over his own shoulder and smile at the memories of Americans grappling with the message of a curious priest who talks too long and speaks with a heavy accent.

"Once I speak in Bakersfield and a man who owns a tire store tells me that if ever I need tires he will give them to me," Father Andrei says. "Eight years later I am back and I need tires. I went to him. He remembered me. He gives me tires. He said he remembered me because my talk was beautiful. So I asked him what I said. He said, 'I don't know. But it was beautiful.'"

Epilogue: The Rogue River still flows swiftly at Trail, and so do the words of Father Andrei Urosov. Cash has been short since mid-1988, and the taxes remain unpaid. A small matter, but a troubling one, even for a man of faith.

“The thing that strikes me most deeply
about this job is that
it humbles your soul.
We're heroes, fallen heroes.
And nobody cares that we can do it.”

Mist
Winter

The Hardest Work There Is

I knew a guy from Newport
His bag was plantin' trees.
You could find him just about any time
Out in a slash pile, down on his knees.
    — *"Tree Planter Blues"*
        Rob Richardson

Easy to forget now. Easy enough with an Everest of beer cans growing against the tent wall and nighttime rain murmuring on the canvas roof and the last of dinner scraped from the stewpots. And with guitars chording loud and today's dirty work clothes steaming dry over the woodstove for tomorrow's duty and Rob belting out the blues and Bob's knee better after a couple of hours on ice. With all of that, easy indeed to forget the kind of day it was. But up on the charcoaled slopes, up amid the leg-grabbing, ankle-twisting, fire-blackened jackstraws of slash that refused to go to ashes in last summer's burn, up where the rain rode the wind down every neck, up there it had been a day to test a man's resolve about this business of planting trees.

Had to get the unit done today, even if it meant working till dark, Dave and Bert had said. So off they'd charged, slipping, sliding, cursing, bickering, laughing, clambering across impossibly steep Coast Range ridges. The new man had folded in the first half hour and was last seen thumbing toward Corvallis. In the midst if it, John Bales paused for a moment. "There's a lot of satisfaction doin' this," he said. "Don't tell anybody. We're supposed to hate it."

Still the rain had come, arrowing out of cold clouds that glowered over the timber on the surrounding hills. And still they planted, packing their sodden tree bags up the flanks and over the spines of hogback ridges, swinging their heavy hoedags into a splattering black mix of ash and mud. And when it was done, they'd smirked at the daylight still left and headed back to the tents.

The tents. A dozen and a half of them squat soddenly in the gloaming. They are mostly olive drab and military surplus and some are as big as small houses. Around them, rain sifts softly through towering firs. Light sneaks out the door flaps to launch glimmers in puddles. Tree planting really isn't done this way anymore. Not in western Oregon. Not in winter. But here they are. In a soggy campsite deep in the rainy hills of the state's upper northwest corner. Miles from anywhere, warm and dry. With beer and food and beer and woodstove warmth and maybe, if somebody will just make the run into Vernonia, even more beer.

"Tent crews used to be more common for tree planters in Oregon," says Dave Maier, one of the outfit's two foremen. "But it rains so much that most crews just work close to home or head for a motel. If you get farther east, there are still quite a few planting crews in tents in Idaho and Montana. Back there you get into places where there aren't any towns for miles. We're in a place like that now.

"Some of the guys here have been together for a long time. They like the tents and they like the money they save. It's the only thing you can do. We're out here where there's not a good-sized town where you're not going to find a motel, much less one that wants to take twenty dirty people."

So they're in the tents, renting space and restrooms and electric power at a county campground deep in the Coast Range, midway between Portland and Astoria. Some of them with their women, even a couple of kids. Working hard, playing hard. Once in a while, fighting hard. Some nights the party ends at two. And reveille's at five.

The crew is two crews, really—Maier's group and Bert Gabbert's bunch brought together for an end-of-the-season planting blitz on logged-off units scattered across the midsection of Columbia County. They work for a Newport outfit called Odin, after the Viking warrior. And, since the late 1970s, the tree planters of Odin have elected to take on some of the most isolated planting jobs in Western Oregon. When housing's not available, they bunk in the tents.

At the campground, extension cords loop like vines through the trees, delivering electricity to some of the tents. The camp has restrooms, but not showers, so one of the cords leads to a shower tent, where planks keep feet out of the mud and a tiny hot water heater breaks the chill. Accommodations in the straw-floored tents range from the small, candlelit unit where Rob Richardson and Lisandra Hansen live, to the rustic plush of "Ozone," the barracks-sized military tent that has five occupants, a dining table, a sofa, a color television, and two woodstoves. The top television attraction is weather forecasts. A prediction for a day with only moderate showers always spawns cheers.

Over a season, the crew ranges from twenty-five to thirty-five planters. The work is grueling. New faces come and go. The itinerant treeplanter's life-style may be the closest approximation to lumber camp life of a century ago.

"When I first started planting in the '70s, I'd crawl in the crummy for the ride up the hill and there'd only be three guys that I knew from yesterday," Gabbert says as the camp eases into its evening routine. "The same thing the next day and the day after that. You'd always have people who thought they could do it, ridiculous people who'd show up wearing powder blue sweaters and carrying umbrellas. Tree planting attracts characters. Maybe you can't be normal and do it. You see a lot of guys who like their alcohol. I've seen guys who go to bed with their muddy jeans and boots still on and who'd just as soon punch you as look at you. And then, every once in a while, you'll have a guy on a crew who's a good planter and you'll find out he's got a master's degree or he's a concert pianist or something like that."

Around the Odin camp, the presence of the women and children who stay at the tents civilizes the place a bit. "Sometimes people ask me how I do it," says Lisandra. "It's really not bad, even in this weather. I watch the stew. I watch the kids. I've got a new Stephen King novel. Tonight, a couple of the guys who are short on money are having dinner with us." Even the children seem to fare well. Melissa Bales, four, who's in camp with her parents and her new bicycle, and Marty Graham, six, who travels with his father, have twenty doting uncles every night when the crew trucks roll back into camp.

"In a way, it's nice having the women and kids," says Bob Reigard, who ices a bad knee every night so he can be back on the slopes the next day. "But it's hard, too. My family's back in Newport. It just reminds me of what I'm missing."

"It's worse than that," says Tim McCarthy as he backs up to the stove and watches his soaked jeans generate steam. "I admit I'm jealous sometimes. Three guys get to come back every night to a warm tent and clean dishes."

Frictions like that are always at work in the camp, a sort of portable small town. Its citizens range from Fred Shulmire, who tents alone by choice, talks tough and frequently brandishes a huge Bowie knife, to Jeffrey Gerdis, a gentle, bearded, philosophical ex-logger who speaks poetically about restoring his karma by giving life to new trees. On this rainy night, with the guitars drawing a crowd in Ozone, the friction produces heat. Richardson and Ray Keffer square off—no one knows why—and punches are exchanged. They're separated quickly. In moments, the outfit's peacemakers cajole them into a handshake, an armistice belied by eyes that glare and glint.

Still, there is enough time for some residual craziness. Talk turns to a season when the whole crew opted for Mohawk haircuts. Scissors and razors emerge. Reigard and Shulmire will face the morning with fierce new hairdos. With four guitarists in camp and two budding songwriters in the crew, plus the arrival of two fresh cases from Vernonia, the party goes on. Tomorrow is another day.

From the songs he writes to the meticulous journal he has kept through all of his years of slogging the muddy slopes, Richardson has been trying to define some underlying meaning in the work of planting. He talks about it as the night wears on. "I've done a lot of jobs. But this is the one. This is the one that I love. The thing that strikes me most deeply about this job is that it humbles your soul. We're heroes, fallen heroes. It's the hardest work there is. You see all these people who try it and can't do it. And nobody knows, nobody cares that we can do it."

Epilogue: The men of Odin still plant trees in some of the loneliest places in Oregon. But, since 1987, the outfit has begun to acquire a reputation as a crack firefighting team. The Odin crews spent six weeks on the lines in the 1988 campaign that became known as "The Battle of Yellowstone."

He is an old, old skipper,
and his memory navigates the
back channels and sloughs
and eddies of a maritime era all but
forgotten on Oregon's south coast.

Allegany
Summer

THE OLD MAN OF THE BAY

THIS IS A STORY of a man and a boat. The man takes his ease in a rocker, clear of gaze, firm of hand, sharp of wit, still well enough to get out for the occasional look at his river now and then. No dry dock for him yet. But for the boat, a very different story.

At memory's helm, the man still can cruise the sloughs and back-channels of a world where boats once counted for more than cars. A button of snuff swells his lower lip and, occasionally, he interrupts the piloting of reminiscences to lean forward and sluice a well-directed shot into the fireplace. Old men are indulged in such things. And Jess Ott is a very, very old man. He is 101.

"The *Welcome*, she was a good boat," he says. "I wore out a half-dozen other ones before I got her. We'd go from here to Marshfield every day. One round-trip a day. Fifty cents one way and six bits a round trip. We'd haul anything—horses, cattle, donkeys, people. She was a good boat."

On the waterfront, there was agreement. "The end of an era," they said, and other things like that, when Jess Ott brought the *Welcome* downriver for the last time almost forty years ago. With dairy farm cream cans stacked on her bow and outgoing mail stashed in her cabin, the forty-eight-footer was a vision out of another time, the last of the fabled mosquito fleet.

It had been a way of life. From puddle-jumping rowboats to car-carrying ferries to bass-whistled sternwheelers. From mail boats to school boats to a church boat. Shall we gather at the river? Everybody did. For almost a century, the mosquito fleet was the underpinning of local commerce and society in the watery region around Coos Bay. Only a look at a map can show why. The Coos River bay area that settlers found on the south coast region in the 1850s was an Oregon Zuider Zee, a low-lying area of swampy flatlands laced by a cat's cradle of sloughs, creeks, and rivers; and flanked by timbered Coast Range hills.

The water—the water that was everywhere in the largest protected inlet between San Francisco and Seattle—shaped life on the bay and on the slopes.

Many of the canyons and the flats, homesteaded though they were, would not have roads until well into the 1920s. Coos Bay itself would not be spanned by a north-south highway bridge until 1936. A dozen small settlements sprung up around the watershed. The largest, Marshfield, would later drop its swampy name and become Coos Bay. But decades — whole lifetimes — would go by before the region's water-based way of life would pass from necessity to novelty to naught. In those years, a man who knew boats and the river, a man who had made the transition from steam to diesel, a man who had spent his whole working life on the twenty-four-mile run from Allegany to Marshfield, was a valued commodity.

"There was lots of low spots on the river," Ott says. "They were almost too low to get over when the tide was out. You'd come in fast, so you'd build up a swell behind you. Then you'd slow down and that swell would catch up with you. And just sort of bump-bump-bump it would take you over the low spot."

All those years of all those boats and all those skippers ended forever on that day in December 1948, when the old man brought the *Welcome* into Coos Bay for the last time. She had been built in 1906 and Ott had purchased her in the 1920s. With his son, Harold, he had kept the *Welcome* going for nearly two decades after roads were punched up the canyons, and for a dozen years after the high steel arches of the Highway 101 bridge spanned the bay.

But the omens were all around them. Had been for years.

"They started putting roads up the river in 1929 and the passenger business just dropped off," recalls Harold. "People were buying cars. The mud flats were full of little boats. People would run them up on the flats and just leave them. And all along the riverbanks you'd see the skeletons of old steamboats, left to rot."

Still, not everyone could own a car in those depression years. And a transportation network to haul freight, livestock, mail, and school pupils had yet to develop. Perhaps, too, there was some affection for the mosquito fleet. The name had been coined by William Holland, a famed boat builder who visited the region and was charmed by its aquatic ways. The fleet had been an intrinsic part of life on the bay since 1853, when settlers began staking claims. Building boats was easier than building roads, so the rivers and sloughs became the area's highways. Whole valleys were homesteaded without roads. Homes and barns were built with every nail, every board hauled upriver by boat. Farm families visited by rowing or sailing from dock to dock in their skiffs.

The water carried all facets of life and commerce, from doctors making house calls to sheriff's deputies serving warrants to mourners seeing coffins to cemeteries. Picnic excursions, with the ladies elegant in long dresses and the gentlemen proper in ties and bowlers, were the high point of the summer social season. The steamboats, big paddlewheelers, were the queens of the rivers. But gasoline and diesel boats, large and small, began supplanting them after 1912.

Jess Ott had broken in on the sternwheeler *Alert,* captained by his father-in-law. Ott was a licensed skipper in his own right by the time he was twenty-one. From there, his life was filled with a series of boats with names like *Cadillac, Coos River, Mecca, Mary Ann* and, finally, the *Welcome*. Ott's regular run was the Coos River's North Fork, known these days as the Millicoma. In addition to hauling freight and passengers, he contracted to deliver mail to farm docks, take children to the Coos River School and transport cream downriver to Coos Bay. On his run from his home at Allegany he often would pick up shopping lists from farm families. When he hit Marshfield, he would drop the lists off at the appropriate hardware and grocery stores. Merchants would box up the orders and deliver them to the docks before Ott headed back upriver. "It was seven days a week," Ott says. "Even holidays. One time I worked seven years without a day off."

Occasionally there was excitement. In 1923, he headed out on an evening run in the *Welcome*. In the cabin below, his wife, Florence, was in labor. "I'd called ahead for the doctor but I knew we weren't going to make it," he says. "So I pulled into one of the farms and picked up an old lady to go along. I stayed up at the wheel. I figured I wasn't going to be much help down below. We met the doctor out in the middle of the river, about a half-hour after the kid was born."

With memories like that, Ott found it hard to let go of the river. He kept the *Welcome* going until the winter of 1948. But six months earlier, he had lost the school contract. By then, the roads that carried the yellow buses were also carrying the people and the freight. The mail contract and the milk cans weren't enough. "There wasn't the money in it anymore," Ott says. "I held on as long as I could. But when it was all over I felt relief. Just relief."

Still, it was a sad day when he sold the *Welcome* a couple of years later. After that, he would hear her name mentioned now and then. He knew that she had been moved to Winchester Bay, had gotten new engines and had her freight-and-passenger topsides peeled away so she could be rebuilt as a tug. Her name, he heard, hadn't changed. And then he lost track. Settled into the rocking chair to dip snuff, watch the weather and enjoy his great-great-grandchildren.

But the *Welcome,* the last boat of the mosquito fleet, sailed on. Purchased by Dewey Abbot of Reedsport, she had indeed been rebuilt with a pair of 100-horsepower diesels and a new tug-style superstructure. For nearly a decade, Umpqua Valley loggers knew her well as she shepherded log rafts down the river. In the early 1970s, Martin Andruss of Winchester Bay bought the vessel. Andruss operated a dock construction business at Winchester Bay. The *Welcome,* often towing a barge with a piledriver used to build docks and piers, remained a familiar sight along the Umpqua.

In 1985, an economic slump caught up with Andruss's small business. He hauled the *Welcome* out of the water and stored her near his home, about a mile from the river. A bit the worse for wear and vandalism, the boat still sits there. And on a hot August day in 1987, Jess Ott comes to pay a call. A carload of relatives, including grown children who had ridden the boat to school and a great-grandchild who has heard stories of the *Welcome* for all of her young life, stand respectfully in the background, reluctant to intrude on his moment, but unwilling to miss it.

Jess Ott, clearly in better repair than his old vessel, runs his hands over the weather-cracked hull, stoops and bends beneath the stern to survey the new twin propellor arrangement. He marvels a bit at seeing the boat so far from water. Some memories come flooding back, including the names of the men who had built the *Welcome.* The old man notes some touches of dry rot, runs his hand over sun-dried joints that gape wide. But memory's picture prevails.

"She was a good boat."

Epilogue: At 103, Jess Ott sat comfortably by the fireplace as the winter of 1988-89 turned to spring. The Welcome *still had dry land beneath her keel.*

Ducking, bobbing, weaving while
veneer sheets whip past,
a few of Oregon's millworkers
play the macho game called busheling.

Vaughn
Summer

Marathon Men

WE'RE MAKING PLYWOOD NOW. Crew Number 4 has it going.

An hour into the shift, they have it cranked from high to overdrive. Wood flys. Sweat glistens on the backs of four necks. Eight hands highball like shuttles in some over-revved wood-weaving loom.

Laddie Crippen whips core sections through the spreader at machine gun speed. Rick Edwards plays the glue-slicked sections like a Vegas blackjack dealer with a million dollars on the table. Doug Muntifering and Ron Dunsing are metronomes running at escape velocity, whipping ten-foot veneer sheets over Edwards' head, flinging chips and scraps aside, sprinting to shove a new cart of veneer into place.

They call it busheling.

It's a timber industry term for piecework. And, in the few Oregon plywood mills where the tradition continues, the guys who do it are likely to be the most cantankerous, single-minded dudes on the floor. Every day it is the shootout at the OK Corral. The winners take home the biggest paycheck and maybe get to chalk their numbers on the wall. We're talking teamwork here, and counting seconds. Five minutes, maybe six, for lunch and a bit less for a pair of breaks during the day. A crew, most often four men, pitted against the clock. And, occasionally, against the boss and against the system.

"Other people, the people who work by the hour, they look at the clock and they want it to go faster," says Dunsing, a busheler for twenty-one years. "But when you're busheling you're always trying to get that clock to slow down. You're always wanting to get out one more load before you have to quit."

Busheling has been part of the Northwest plywood industry for more than sixty years. But the concept took hold after 1950 in southern Oregon, then spread to many of the mills around the state. The most typical arrangement was that a core-layup and glue-spreading team worked on the busheling plan, while all other jobs in the mill were paid at an hourly rate. For mill operators, the attraction of the arrangement was that a good busheling crew might out-produce hourly workers by 25 to 50 percent. For the bushelers, the draw was that their paychecks would be substantially larger.

Bushelers, at least in their own eyes, were the cream of the crop, the crews who worked with ferocity and always took home the biggest paychecks. They were not necessarily loved by hourly workers. They did not necessarily care.

"Busheling crews have always been the prima donnas of plywood," says Wayne Pape, plywood division manager for Bohemia, Inc. "With the good ones, there's just a lot of pride. When they have a big day, they put the number on the wall, for everybody to see it. Sometimes, when they quit, all four of them will pick up and go at once. It used to be common for them to move any time there was a mill down the road that paid three cents more. Over the years some of them even walked away from good retirement plans to do that. That's the way a busheler was."

It is not quite like that anymore. Even a busheler is likely to keep one eye on his fringe benefit package. And there simply are not as many mills out there to snap up a good busheler or an entire crew. Many of the plywood mills of the 1980s have automated, turning the core-laying and veneer-slinging jobs over to machines. But the Northwest still counts some plants where busheling continues, where high-speed crews work to stretch the clock every day. Usually busheling crews are found in mills that have not automated because they produce a varying mix of panel sizes and grades. One of those plants is Bohemia Inc.'s Vaughn plywood mill, where Crew Number 4 is ranked as the mill's best busheling team.

Number 4 is a typical collection of Oregon bushelers. When they are working they don't talk much, not among themselves and certainly not to an outsider. The time for talking is an hour before the shift starts, or better yet an hour after, with hands wrapped around a beer. Each man on the crew has worked with at least one of the others in another time, another place.

"I've worked in more mills than I am years old," says Dunsing, who is forty-four. "You're always chasing that rainbow, always looking for that perfect job. If you're good, it's never any problem. You won't even miss a day between jobs. People come looking for you."

"I got mad at a foreman once, so I quit and went to a tavern," says Muntifering, who is forty-two. "Before I finished my second beer, I got two calls for jobs. Another place, they wouldn't give one guy on our crew a fifty dollar draw on his check. So all four of us walked out. We got other jobs right away."

These days a busheling crew is paid 95 cents to $1.18 per thousand square feet of plywood core that it lays. In a typical rectangular sheet of plywood, the outer faces always have grain that runs the length of the sheet. Core material has the grain running crosswise. A three-ply panel has one layer of core. A seven-ply has three core layers, alternating with four sheets of lengthwise grain. A seven-ply, four-by-eight-foot panel puts ninety-six square feet of core on the production tally.

On a busheling crew, the members split the take from their work equally, an arrangement that makes crews self-regulating mechanisms. "You almost never have to fire a busheler for production reasons," says Dennis Ferguson, the mill's superintendent. "The other three guys on that crew will always take care of it. They know if one guy is screwing up, they're losing money. They'll see to it he doesn't last. And if we need a replacement, they know who'll be good."

The bushelers of Crew Number 4 all expect annual earnings somewhere over $30,000 these days. But they have known better years, when the core rate was up to $1.44 in the days before the lumber industry's pay rollbacks of the 1980s. Each man on the crew can remember a year over $40,000 and Muntifering once hit $47,000. Some say that busheling is a young man's job. The industry rule of thumb once was that a worker could stand the pace for ten years or until age forty, whichever came first. But Crew Number 4 has three workers over forty, and all of them like to talk about fifty-five-year-old bushelers they have known.

"The better the wood, the longer you can last," says Crippen, forty-five, a twenty-three-year busheling veteran. "You seldom find a busheling mill where the veneer quality is as good as it is here. You need good wood to make good money if you're going to do this."

In every mill there is a crew production record. The number represents the optimum output. Because equipment varies from one mill to the next, production records will also vary significantly. In most plants, the crew record will be chalked on the wall or spray-painted defiantly on some overhead beam. All four of the bushelers on Number 4 have set records in other mills. Two members of the Number 4 bunch helped push the Vaughn record to 147,480 feet of core. The present crew has its sights set on ramming the mark past 160,000. "You just pick a day when everything looks right," Dunsing says. "And then you let it all hang out. We could get it past 160,000 on the right day. It'll happen."

Plant capacity, especially in the plywood heat-laminating presses, is usually the limitation on a record attempt. The all-time industry record was set by a busheling bunch a few years back at Sutherlin. A beefed-up crew shoved out a mark that is expected to stand for years. "It was 235,008," says Edwards, who is thirty-one. "I worked in that mill for a while. They had a big sign up with that number. It was the first thing you saw. I've never forgotten it."

For bushelers, the non-stop pace becomes a way of life. Edwards has not taken a day off in five years, and Dunsing has missed only one in the last three. Even mowing lawn or splitting firewood on weekends, bushelers are likely to start after breakfast and not quit until dinner.

"A few years ago, I got to worrying about what I was going to do when I was too old to do this," Crippen says. "So I got myself a good job driving truck. I couldn't stand it. I was absolutely bored."

Epilogue: On July 11, 1988, Crew Number 4 shoved the Vaughn plant production record to 147,800. Seeking a schedule with free weekends, Ron Dunsing has since joined another busheling crew at the mill. On Oct. 8, 1988, a crew of graveyard shift bushelers at Vaughn ran the record to 159,680 feet.

T his livelihood that Mel Lentz pursues
is a frontierish sport,
one that has flowered only
on the frontierish continents of
North America and Australia.

Creswell
Summer

LOGGIN' MAN

Perhaps the secret is only a matter of muscle and sinew, of human geometry and physics applied to the task at hand. Perhaps it springs from the endless hours of grinding, filing, honing—the primeval role of Man the Toolmaker ever seeking the new edge sharper and finer than the last. Or perhaps the answer is even more elemental, rooted in that facet of humanity which assures that, as soon as a human runs a mile or swims a river or skis a hill or drives a car or sails a boat, another will try to do it faster.

But hints of other answers glint in the chips and the sawdust and the world records that avalanche from the bit of Mel Lentz's axe and the teeth of his saws. There is enough in this ultimate timber beast, this woods warrior who talks like L'il Abner and swings an axe like Paul Bunyan, to add a ton of fuel to the debate on the influences of heredity and environment and opportunity.

Is Mel Lentz America's top competitive logger because he is the son of Merv Lentz and the grandson of Ben, who each yarded in titles for years? Or is Mel, who seems destined to eclipse all his forebears' records, on that track because he grew up so close to the tools of the woods that he was competing before he was twelve? Or is it simply that Lentz, seasoned by years of overseas competition and the undivided attention of an Aussie coach who has chosen to make a Yank the repository of his own considerable skills, has fortuitously fallen into a situation that gives him the best of both worlds?

"He's become the standard by which you judge competition logging," says Ray Poppe of Arlington, Washington, a former champion and president of a record-keeping body called the Worldwide Association of Timber Sports. "It's simply amazing what he has accomplished at his age. When you look, you can see that everything was there. His grandfather and his father were champions before him. He grew up with it. Then he gets Jim Alexander helping him with everything the Australians know. Everything has come together in one person. It's just a thrill to watch every time he steps up to go to work."

At twenty-seven, Mel Lentz is a veteran in a realm of sport where men often do not come of age until they are thirty and where the best may remain competitive until they approach fifty. Some say he seems poised to dominate competition logging well into the next century, if the road and the pace of a life-style that spans two hemispheres do not get to him first.

It is a frontierish sport, this livelihood of his, and one that has truly flowered only on the frontier continents of North America and Australia. From Nova Scotia to British Columbia, from Maine to Oregon, from Queensland to Tasmania, the demanding work of the woods has been translated into a search for those who can chop it, saw it, throw it, and climb it the fastest. "I was eleven when I started," Mel says. "I was going to shows with my dad all the time. I started doing some axe-throwing. That was the only thing they'd let you do when you were that young. After a few years, I was winning some."

During that same period, his father was winding up an unparalleled competitive career, winning twelve all-around logger titles at Hayward, Wisconsin, and at the Albany, Oregon, Timber Carnival, the two top events in the United States. By age sixteen, the son was handling one end of a crosscut saw and turning in credible performances. At age seventeen, he placed second in national competition at Hayward; at eighteen he won a title.

In those years Mel was holding up his end, too, on Creswell's high school basketball team. At six-feet-four, he averaged more than twenty-six points a game as a senior and had some college coaches looking. He tested that road for a year in junior college. But success was coming too quickly in the arenas where chain saws screamed and chips and sawdust flew. "I just found out I was doing good enough that I could make money at it," he says. "I really wanted to find out what I could do with it. My dad had quit. We never competed against each other. But I wanted to see how far I could go with it."

In 1979, Mel committed himself to full-time competition, to seeing if he could become one of the four or five loggers in the world to earn a living matching his skills against others. In the winter of that year, he headed for Australia. Even before that, he had fallen under the tutelage of Alexander, a legendary Australian who had been a top competitor in both the United States and the Southern Hemisphere. Alexander and Lentz's father had set records in the United States as teammates in crosscut saw competition.

Alexander had watched Mel grow from boy to man-child and he was awed at the potential he saw. In Australia, he took Lentz in tow and began turning his years of experience to the task of teaching a nineteen-year-old Oregonian how to beat the Australians and the New Zealanders at their own games on their own turf. "I couldn't find anyone to work with in my country," Alexander says. "A lot of the competition there is father and son. What dad does, the son does. What dad believes, the son believes. It's hard to convince anyone there might be a better way."

As much as any other modern coach, Alexander is an analyst of both physical and mental skills. He compares the perfect axe stroke or the perfect crosscut saw rhythm to the perfect golf swing. He speaks of the motion of the axe through wood

Balanced precariously on an old-fashioned logging springboard and alternately chopping with right- and left-handed swings, Mel Lentz can whip his axe through a twelve-inch log in seconds.

as if the tool were a complex device composed of multiple moving parts. He talks about the mind game—preparation, concentration, visualization of performance. Alexander still competes in a few chopping events, although he has lost a second or two over the years.

At Albany a few seasons ago, Lentz was wrapping up his sixth all-around title in as many years. In the process, the student wiped out the last of the teacher's world records. To do it, he whipped an axe through a horizontal fourteen-inch log in a shade over twenty-two seconds. Always thoughtful but seldom eloquent, more given to talking with his tools than his mouth, Lentz capped that chopping performance by facing the stands and paying tribute to Alexander, who at that point had invested more than seven years in schooling his protege. Those who saw it remember that Alexander was visibly moved. "A record is only made to be broken," he says. "I'm pleased that he broke it. It shows that what I've been telling him is getting through."

In Australia, where Lentz lives up to seven months a year and spends virtually every weekend in an arena, competitive logging is a major attraction. In each of the Australian states, regional competitions known as royal shows fill huge arenas. The Australian competition is limited to chopping and hand-sawing events. Those skills are the foundation of American competition, which is expanded with events in tree climbing, choker setting, obstacle courses, chainsaw cutting and log rolling, or birling. Because events are staged differently—with variations in factors such as axe size, log diameter, and native woods—Australia, the United States, and Canada offer a variety of world titles in their competitions. As in rodeo or track, contestants choose their events. Lentz does them all, except for climbing and log rolling. His schedule for the five months that he spends in the United States each year is almost as heavy as his Australian itinerary. But it is Australia that has defined his skills and pushed him to his limits.

"I went to Australia for the competition," says the axman from Oregon. "I wasn't going to get any better at home. In the States, I can go to a really big show and there's maybe only one guy—someone like Roland Eslinger from California—who's going to push me. At a big competition in Australia, there may be seven or eight guys who are really good."

Lentz spent some years paying his dues in Australia. He won grudging and, later, genuine respect from Australia's thousands of knowledgeable competition logging fans. In 1985, he took a world title in a chopping event in Sydney. In the emotional moment that followed, the Aussie fans paid tribute to the Yank who had beaten their best. In recent years, Lentz has won eight Australian titles in various individual chopping and sawing events. Back in North America, he has taken seven consecutive all-around titles at Albany and four at Hayward. For good measure, he has won the Canadian world championship all three times that the event has been staged in the 1980s.

When he is competing on the North American continent, Lentz uses his home town of Creswell as a base. One of his haunts is the shop of knifemaker Bill Harsey, where Lentz, Alexander, and Harsey spend hours honing the competition tools Mel will carry into battle. More of that work goes on in the shop where the Lentz family's log trucking operation is based. It is there, watching the sparks fly from the grinder, that Lentz talks most freely about the life he has chosen for himself.

"This is what makes it a full-time job," he says as he guides a loop of saw chain through the machine. "It's nothing to put in a fourteen-hour day out here. I take every chain apart. Every link. I take fifteen thousandths of an inch off each piece. I put it all back together, grind off the rivets, and then start working on sharpening it. It can take anywhere from twenty-five to forty hours a chain. I take four chains to a show. And that's just one piece of the work. It's all like that. It's hours and hours in the shop for every minute you're up there competing."

The money for such effort is respectable, but it is not phenomenal. After covering the heavy costs of equipment and travel, Lentz nets something over $30,000 a year. Placing in seven or eight events and taking the all around title at a big competition such as Albany or Hayward can be worth over $3,000. Doing equally well in one of the major Australian shows can net him as much as $6,000. But between the big shows are scores of small ones where, even if Lentz sweeps all the events he enters, he is lucky to come away with $500.

"I think I'm really strongest in the basic chopping and sawing stuff," Mel admits. "When I'm in Australia, that's all they do. No chain saws. Down there, I can really concentrate on those things, and I have Jim working with me. I'd say I'm weaker in the chain saw events."

Weak is relative. In the United States, Lentz holds a world record of 7.8 seconds for screaming through a thirty-inch log with a built-from-scratch competition saw powered by a motorcycle engine. Burning an exotic racing fuel, weighing sixty pounds, and cranking out forty horsepower, the monster saw has three times the heft and seven times the output of a typical logger's saw. The new record he set with the machine was a stunning eight-tenths of a second below the previous record, which he had posted a year earlier.

Working with Alexander has made Lentz more analytical about the demands of competition and the peculiar requirements of each of the ten or so events in which he competes. But Shirley Smith, his long-time partner in the Jack and Jill event which teams a man and a woman on a crosscut saw, knows that analysis goes only so far with Lentz. "I used to compete with my brother," Smith says. "He would always figure what we were going to do, exactly how fast we were going to cut to win. Mel is completely different. You can tell he does a lot of thinking about what's going on out there. And then he'll just say that, no matter what happens, we're gonna cut it faster than anybody else does."

Epilogue: Mel Lentz extended his string of Albany Timber Carnival championships with wins in 1987 and 1988. During those years, he also set new handsawing records in Australia. At Hayward, Wisconsin, in 1987, he established a new world record by whipping an axe through a fourteen-inch block of white pine in 22.05 seconds.

Hewing to traditions, chasing fancies, saving what is precious, some among us are brave enough to follow their own compasses.

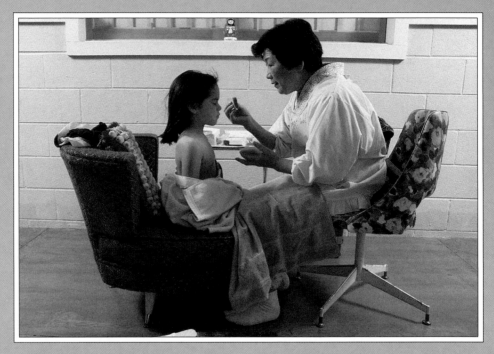

VISIONARIES, ZEALOTS, AND CHARACTERS

There is something in this more than natural
— SHAKESPEARE

DREAMWEAVERS AND RAINBOW CHASERS and windmill tilters and champions of ideas, I love them all. Clarence Darrow, the dean of trial lawyers, once said that with a jury of Irishmen he could get Judas off with a five dollar fine. The journalist's corollary is that, with a zealot, he has every chance of delivering a good story even on a bad day.

They come packaged all ways, these Oregonians who order their lives around a singular commitment to an idea or a way of living. Some are out there waging battles the rest of us wish we had the courage to fight, preserving things of value, living in ways that are instructive to us all. Some pose questions that give us pause. And a few soar in their own fragile orbits, intersecting reality as fleetingly as a stone skipping across a pond, but still creating ripples that shimmer and delight.

Too often, I have been guilty of the reporter's sin: I have approached their stories with flimsy preconceptions, only to come away marveling at what I have found and questioning my ability to do it justice.

I went to do a simple bread-and-butter piece on a man who trains sheepdogs, and found new perspectives on the elemental matter of choosing a life's work. Going in, I thought I had the number of the latter-day frontiersman dressed in buckskins, but he proved to be serious and academic, devoted in the most professional way to mastering the skills of a way of life that flourished long before the white man came. The old man living by choice in the ramshackle house at river's edge knew more about aging with style — forget about grace, he would say — than a gaggle of retirement consultants.

The writer John McPhee says that the certainty in writing is that your work will be read by people who know far more than you. And if luck is with you, your sources are the same sort of people.

On a bluff above the ocean,
a man set himself to the task
of rebuilding nature's shattered creatures
and, in the process,
reconstructed his own life.

Bandon
Winter

THE BIRDMAN OF BANDON

THEY LIVE TOGETHER in a house down by the ocean, the one-winged hawk and the blind owl and the walking gull and the soft-handed man with the steel brace armoring his leg.

Damaged goods, to be sure. Paying with a lifetime for their encounters with man and his weapons and his machines. War vets, all of them, in a sense. For Dan Deuel, the man with the gnarled legs and the step-and-a-half gait, the scars of body and mind run deep. From mine fields and helicopter crashes and dead friends and caustic memories of Vietnam. From surviving it all, only to stand at a California roadside and take a direct hit from a seventy-mph drunken driver. From marriages that failed. From pain that never stops, medical treatments that never end.

But this house by the ocean is about survival, not bitterness. Every occupant arrives in pain, and far too many—hawks, owls, murres, gulls, eagles, even hummingbirds—will die there, despite the man's best efforts. Nonetheless, the place is pervaded with a humor that at times is checkreined just short of zaniness.

Of course. The rehabilitator-in-residence used that medicine above all others in his own case. It was laughter that kept him going in the dark months after they scraped his broken body up from the highway and made him a textbook case in the New England Journal of Medicine. Learned to imitate his surgeon's voice, he did, so that he could phone the nurses' station late at night and order up extra massages and conversation and food for the patient.

"Sometimes," says Deuel, forty, "I'll walk out and look at the ocean and the birds and I'll feel so good I'll jump off the porch. All of a sudden I'm up in the air and I'm looking down at my brace and my legs. . . . It's crash time. First they said I was going to die. Then I was going to be a vegetable. After a while, you get a little devil-may-care. I do what I need to do to keep this going. Why not? What are they going to do to me now? Draft me and send me to a war? Hit me with a car?"

They most assuredly are not. In Bandon, they talk about Dan Deuel the way the Japanese speak of those rare individuals identified as national treasures. The word gets around that the birdman is short of money, and a benefit jazz concert materializes, with community groups jumping in to help raise a couple of thousand dollars. And along the West Coast, professionals like Peter Howorth, director of the Marine Mammal Center at Santa Barbara, California, are coming to respect the accomplishments of Deuel and of Free Flight, the non-profit bird rehabilitation operation he started on a shoestring in 1976.

"Oregon would be a poorer place without him," Howorth says. "He's made himself a gifted rehabilitation worker. I've been up numerous times to see what he's doing and I have nothing but the highest respect for his work."

In Deuel's Southern California boyhood there were some pet birds. After high school, he squeezed in some college courses in wildlife management. He was less than a dedicated student. "The war in Vietnam was going on, but I wasn't paying much attention," he says. "I was young, confused. I had other things on my mind. I played Bob Dylan's music but I never listened to the words."

A draft notice increased his attention level. He wound up in Vietnam, providing combat intelligence for the First Air Cavalry Division. It was work that often shoved him into combat zones, traveling alone with a Vietnamese interpreter. He left Vietnam with two Bronze Stars, a Purple Heart, and an Air Medal. He does not talk much about the decorations.

"I got mine because I was white and because somebody happened to be watching," he says. "The really hairy stuff happened when there weren't any witnesses. My outlook really changed in those years. It shows in the letters I wrote. When I started I was a man, a killer, a stud. By the time it was over I wasn't sure why we were there. I knew I could die. I grew up. That was the big thing about that war. It was different. A lot of people like to call us whiners, but it wasn't like any of the other wars."

He married while he was finishing his Army hitch. Back in California, he landed a job as a department store security chief. Headed home from work one evening on his motorcyle, he stopped to aid another motorcyclist stalled at roadside. Deuel had just dismounted at the edge of the freeway when the drunk in the car nailed him. His pelvis and legs were shattered. His internal injuries included a tear of the aorta, the body's main blood vessel. "I was in a coma for a long time," he says. "I made the medical journals as the first person ever to survive a heart-lung bypass on a thing called the Bramson heart-lung machine."

At one point, his weight dropped to eighty-six pounds. He was left with two damaged legs, including one that would always require a brace, and with a propensity for seizures, which he controls with medication. He learned to walk again, but his gait would never be normal. After his release from the hospital, his wife asked for a divorce. Over the next two years there was a modest insurance settlement, a new marriage, and a decision to move to Oregon. He used the settlement to buy a small, old house in an oceanfront section of Bandon.

"One night I decided to go to a lecture," he says. "It was an Audubon Society thing or something like that. And there were some people there with a golden eagle and owls and a hawk. I was in awe. It was dynamite. The lights came on for me right there." By 1977, Deuel had himself certified as a rehabilitation specialist, authorized to treat injured wild birds. Then he organized Free Flight as a nonprofit corporation and established a link with Dr. Joe Pettit, a Bandon veterinarian who advises him and who makes his own contribution to Deuel's work by providing surgical treatment for the birds.

Initially, Deuel thought that he would get, perhaps, a few oil-soaked murres during the winter storm season. But the volume of cases expanded dramatically as word of his work spread along the south coast. State Police game officers, farmers, loggers, and motorists showed up more and more often at his door. The birds they brought ranged from eagles to hummingbirds. Almost always they were man's victims — hit by a car, shot by a hunter, damaged by a piece of plastic or metal litter. Deuel's skills grew. He learned to set broken wings, dress wounds, provide intravenous therapy, and manage demanding feeding schedules.

It is remorseful work. He treats up to four hundred birds a year. The survival rate is about 40 percent. Although he keeps two one-winged birds from some early amputation cases, birds requiring such treatment now are destroyed. The same fate awaits the growing number of red-tailed hawks who lose their legs or wings because they are attracted to the bait in traps set for four-footed game. "You can amputate a hawk's wing and you can keep him alive," Deuel says. "But he still thinks he's a hawk and he still trys to fly. It's not much fun."

The phone in the little house by the ocean rings at all hours. Usually Deuel asks callers to deliver the injured birds they find. But he will fire up his ancient Volvo if the injury case is a difficult-to-handle hawk, pelican, or eagle.

Deuel's second marriage ended in divorce in 1984. He survives on Social Security disability payments. The work of Free Flight goes on, supported by less than $10,000 in annual donations. Deuel ranges the coast, speaking as a bird advocate to school groups, college classes, service clubs, and tourist sessions in state parks. He is assisted in most of the work by Mary Crumley, a Bandon resident and close friend. Aided by Bandon volunteers who worked non-stop for thirty-two days, they once nursed to health an abandoned harbor seal pup, too young to feed itself, and saw it successfully return to the sea.

Others help in their own ways. "Happens all the time," Deuel says. "You're just dressed up and ready to go someplace and you look out the window and there's a game cop dumping a dead elk on the driveway. That's a lot of bird food. The only thing you can do is go out and start cutting it up for the freezer."

The task of adjusting to the memories of war goes on too, reduced to manageable proportions but never completely out of mind. Deuel still recalls the dates when friends died. For him, the violence of that time and the work of putting nature's creatures back on the wing are all of a piece. The life-taker has become a lifesaver. In the fall of 1986, when the traveling replica of the Vietnam Veterans Memorial was in Eugene, he took his medals, some photos of his birds and a summation of his thoughts to the wall. He left them there and walked away.

"On a daily basis I see creatures that were hurt for no reason except that they encountered man," he says. "In a way, that's what happened to me, too. But I've taken the war experience and the accident experience and I've tried to make something out of them in what I do.

"It's like a tree. Those are my growth rings."

Epilogue: Since 1987, Dan Deuel's efforts have expanded to include rehabilitation work with abandoned seals and sea lion pups. Donations have enabled him to convert a portion of his small home to an intensive care ward for animals.

He is short, stout, and zealous,
a man who, when the topic is music,
can preach with the conviction
and the zeal
of a tent-meeting evangelist.

Klamath Falls
Autumn

THE KEEPER OF THE MUSIC

GENE AUTRY IS IN THE BATHROOM, stacked five feet high. Lionel Hampton and Rudy Valee live in jumbled splendor with a thousand other artists on the glassed-in front porch. Ton upon ton, Glenn Miller and Hank Williams and Chuck Berry and Rosemary Clooney and Guy Lombardo and Ann Murray share what was once a living room. Over it all, the voice of Elvis laughs, sings, jokes, swears as he and a group of studio musicians struggle to produce a zero defect "Can't Help Falling in Love." Down the wall, an album-cover Enrico Caruso leans out of a crazily canted shelf to survey the whole improbable scene.

Stanley Kilarr keeps house with the lot of them. Generous host that he is at seventy-two, he takes precious little of his home for himself. The keeper of half a million records lives on tiny trails that wander off like rabbit runs through stacks of albums, leaning towers of plastic and cardboard that seem poised to create the ultimate musical avalanche.

A trail to the bed. A trail to the tub. A clearing, but a small one, in the kitchen where Kilarr spends most of his waking hours. The rest is records. Gutbucket blues players and Czechoslovakian sopranos. Crooners from the 1940s and rockers from the 1960s. All of them heaped together as if some great glacier had shoved a century of music before it and deposited the whole unlikely melodic moraine in a ramshackle house in Klamath Falls. The couch and the easy chair were buried beneath recorded history about 1951. The floors buckled long ago, sagging more than a foot in some spots to touch the earth beneath them. The mail waits, a year deep, on the kitchen table. The floor is stacked with bachelor staples—canned chili, tomato soup, potato chips.

"It's all organized, really," Kilarr is saying as he leads the tour. "I can find anything here. It may take a week or so but I'll have it and I'll find it. I get my nephews in here to help me move the stacks. Sometimes we have to take big stacks out in the yard so we've got room to dig out what we need. I do tapes for all kinds of people. But older people, mostly. They want the music they remember. They write and ask me for copies. I'm a year behind on the mail but I almost always find what they want."

He is short, stout, and zealous, a man who, when the topic is music, can preach with the conviction and the duration of a tent-meeting revivalist. If there were record-album liner notes on this life, they would tell the story of a man who developed a consuming addiction for recorded sound at the age of eight, as a newspaper carrier in Portland. One of the boy's customers was a Greek who ran a fruit stand, spoke almost no English, and played a record of "Yes, We Have No Bananas" without cease. The boy bought a copy of the record from the Greek and was on his way. By the time Kilarr was a teenager, most homes had radios. Americans who only a few years earlier had considered records the ultimate in home entertainment were moving phonographs to the attic.

"People were just getting rid of them," Kilarr says. "I started going house to house. I'd ask people for their old records. They were happy to get rid of them. By the time I was sixteen, I had so many that my folks told me to either get rid of them or move them out. So I rented a little place to store them. And I started throwing away stuff I really didn't like. Oh, I threw away things I wish I'd kept. I got rid of some early Negro blues stuff that was just amazing — because I was a kid then and it didn't interest me."

Later, Kilarr's family lived in Klamath Falls and he came to consider the city his home, even though he did not live there regularly for decades. Through most of his adult life, Kilarr worked as a gambling table dealer in Nevada. Through all of it, he collected records. He haunted auctions and record warehouses, spent vast amounts of his earnings on music, became a familiar figure in collectors' circles. In the 1950s, someone in that circle, noting his passion for anything recorded in the United States by anybody, dubbed him "Mr. Americana." The moniker has stuck. Sometimes, mail from European or Australian collectors arrives addressed only to "Mr. Americana, Klamath Falls, Oregon."

"When I was working in Reno, I never went out to party around like other guys," he says. "I just took my check and went looking for records. There were some places in San Francisco that I went to every three weeks. I had this place rented in Klamath Falls. About every five weeks I'd drive up here with a Cadillac full of records and store them. Sometimes old people would tell me about some singer I'd never heard of. So I'd start looking. When I found him, I'd buy him."

There were a couple of wives along the way, too. But both of them tired of playing second fiddle to records and moved on. When musical tastes changed, Kilarr's collection expanded accordingly. The dawning of the rock music era, for example, simply gave him new game to hunt.

"Elvis. I really like Elvis," he says. "I didn't care for him much at first. But I listened a while and I figured out that the guy was really a performer. He's my favorite rock singer. He really had it. But I've got 'em all from the '50s and '60s. I've got your Beatles, your Rolling Stones, your Led Zeppelins. All those guys. The rock stuff up to the mid-'70s was pretty good. But as far as I'm concerned there hasn't been anything good done in the last ten years. I don't bother with it."

Kilarr also wove an extensive network among the producers and sellers of bootleg recordings — unauthorized sound tracks from concerts and recording sessions, or copies of old material still under copyright. He purchased whatever

VISIONARIES, ZEALOTS, AND CHARACTERS

was available. The collector retired a few years ago and came home to live with his collection. The major portion of it is crammed into the small house in Klamath Falls, although several thousand records are still in storage in Reno.

He lives these days on Social Security and continues to expand the collection by charging a small fee for copy tapes. "Sometimes it can take me a week to find the record and get the copy made," Kilarr says. "I work on that stuff every day. It keeps me alive." He and a few other collectors around the country are regular resources for television networks and recording companies. Studios often did not save master tapes, so producers rely on the collectors when making documentaries, records, or tapes of old music.

All of the money that Kilarr earns from the sale of tapes goes back into the collection. He is still buying records, including antique Edison cylinder recordings, and also has branched into early sheet music. His biggest concern these days is the future of his collection. A few buyers have expressed interest and a couple of universities have indicated they would be willing to accept the collection if Kilarr would offer it. But Kilarr has a larger vision. He wants a museum. Occasionally, he fires off letters in search of grant money.

"All I want is a quarter-million dollars," he says. "I'd get ten acres somewhere around here and have the place sort of like an old farm. About two-thirds of it would be for the records and music. The rest would be for old silent films. I don't want to break up the collection. It's my brainchild. I'd like to set up a corporation of young kids. They could take it over and keep it going—make it bigger. Two hundred years from now, this music would still be here.

"I've put a lifetime into this. I want to leave behind something that's beautiful."

Epilogue: Since 1987, Stanley Kilarr has refused what he describes as a seven-figure offer for his collection. But he continues to seek a museum grant from corporations and foundations. His collection grows, with hundreds of recent additions donated by Americans who have heard and read of his work.

Like a keeper of the flame,
Kanriye Fujima passes on to Oregon children
the precious art
she has brought from a faraway land
across the sea.

Ontario
Autumn

THE TRADITIONALIST

Aɴʏ Aᴍᴇʀɪᴄᴀɴ ᴋɪᴅ who has taken piano lessons would understand. It was a hot day in Japan, and a young girl, whose parents were seeing to it that she grew up versed in the culture of her land, headed out the door for her music lesson. But the sun was too enticing. She tossed her three-stringed wooden samisen onto the roof and headed off to the neighborhood swimming hole. The water was fine. But the delicate, banjo-like instrument was not. The hot afternoon sun warped it into uselessness—with predictable parental consequences.

That was more than fifty years ago. Kanriye Fujima laughs now as she tells the story from her early years of training in traditional Japanese dance and music. The laughter and the smiles come frequently when she spins out the unlikely, engaging tale of her working life. It is an account that moves halfway around the globe, from the structured master-and-pupil dance regimen of prewar Japan to another "Far East," the sagebrush country of eastern Oregon. Threading through the story is Fujima's dedication to an ancient art—the traditional Japanese dance forms—coupled with an unflagging thirty-year commitment to pass the traditions on to the children of American Japanese.

"I have never had children," she says. "But I have lots of children, in three cities—Portland, Spokane, and here. All of my students are my children."

From Ontario, Fujima—she is Madame Fujima to her students—each year drives the thousands of miles to teach her classes, making the long trips down the Columbia Gorge to Portland or across southeastern Washington's Palouse country to Spokane. The classes, which number about twenty-five students in each city, have grown a bit smaller over the years, reflecting some erosion of interest in preserving the old ways. But still there are many Japanese-Americans who want their children to learn not only the traditional culture but the attitudes and rituals and rigorous standards of performance that go with learning it. And these days, with an emerging American interest in the dances of other cultures, she sees an occasional Caucasian in her classes.

One of them has been Barbara Sellers, a prominent folk dance instructor in Eugene. Sellers, who works at expanding her knowledge of ethnic dances, tracked down Madame Fujima in Portland. The search was worth the effort.

"She is a wonderful teacher," Sellers says. "She's a tremendous blend of the traditional and modern in her approach. She's very knowledgeable and very warm. I'd go into her classes feeling really nervous and maybe a little bit out of place. She has this way of focusing on you and making absolutely certain that you understand. She doesn't just show you the stuff and leave you on your own."

On the road, Madame Fujima gives her classes in the homes of students or former students. Typically, she runs the classes in Spokane and Portland from March until November, showing up in each city for one week out of every month. In the winter months, when storms sweep along the Columbia River Gorge, bad weather and bad roads combine to make it difficult to keep a schedule, so she teaches only in Ontario. Frequently, her Portland students trek there for lessons during the off-season.

Madame Fujima's schedule also includes an annual visit to Japan, where she spends a month working with teachers at the school where she learned her art. She is recognized now as a master, a teacher and performer of both Japanese classical and folk dances and modern Japanese dance, which is based on contemporary Japanese music.

Like many of her students, she found her way into dance with a firm parental push. "When I was small, I saw dancers in a parade," she says. "I liked it. That is why I started. Then I found out it was hard, hard, hard. Then I didn't like the work. But my mother was pushing me. And my stepfather, he pushed me very much. He told me that it would not be enough to be a dancer. I had to become a teacher, if I wanted to succeed. I hated it when he pushed me. But now, I understand."

Fujima's education in the centuries-old classic and folk dances of Japan started when she was six, a rigorous schedule of lessons that began after the end of her regular school day. At first, the lessons included both music and dance. But gradually her training came to focus only on dance. The winds of World War II swept in and brought a halt to her training when she was fifteen. Not until after the war, when she was in her early twenties, did she resume her dance studies, under circumstances that made the old schoolgirl regimen seem easy. She left home to serve under one dancing master and then another. In the traditional way, she paid for her training and also served as a cook, housekeeper, baby sitter, and maid in the master's home. After four years, she was certified as a teacher and began taking in students of her own in Hiroshima and Yamaguchi.

Already, some nontraditional forces were at work on her. In the prewar days, traditional Japanese dance had been carefully segmented among specialists who handled makeup or costumes or choreography. But the system had been disrupted by the war and Kanriye Fujima, the young teacher, often found herself doing all the work. She came to prefer it that way. "I wanted to do all the things that went with the dance," she says. "I wanted to do the weaving and the kimonos and the makeup. After the war I got to do more things, but not all the time."

By the early 1950s, friends who had visited the United States were telling her that she might find a ready market for her skills and her preferred teaching approach. On the other side of the Pacific were thousands of Japanese-American families who wanted their children to grow up with an understanding of the old culture and its traditions. One of those friends also mentioned her name to Etaro Takaki of Portland. Takaki found her in Japan, and they were married in 1956.

"He promised that when I came to America I could do the dance and I could teach children the dancing," Madame Fujima says. "That was most important. It was the big reason I wanted to come to this country." Within months of moving to Portland with her new husband, she had classes under way in that city and in Ontario, which had emerged from the World War II era with a sizable Japanese-American population. And, of necessity, she handled all parts of both the teaching and the performing processes.

Takaki died about a year later. Fujima returned to Japan for a few months, but then decided that, even without a husband, her life's work would be teaching dance to Japanese-American children. She returned to Portland and resumed teaching. From the first of her visits to Ontario, her work there had gotten enthusiastic support from Minoru Fujita, a local restaurant owner. When she reopened her classes in the eastern Oregon town, he continued to back her efforts. They were married in 1960, and she moved to Ontario, maintaining her professional name, Kanriye Fujima.

With her new husband's assistance she was introduced to the Japanese-American community in Spokane and added that city to her barnstorming teaching itinerary. The course of her work was set for the next twenty-five years. Through that period, her husband, who died in 1985, backed her efforts.

"Always he helped," Madame Fujima says. "Without him it would not have been possible. Because of him I could go to Portland or Spokane whenever I wanted. Sometimes, after he retired, he would go with me. But many times he was home alone while I was teaching."

At sixty-four, Madame Fujima intends to continue her teaching work indefinitely. But she performs only rarely now. Friends say it takes a special event such as the wedding of a former student or the visit of a Japanese diplomat to Ontario to get her into makeup and on stage.

The parents of her students count themselves lucky. "My daughters are at Oregon State now," says Susie Nishihara, who is now a Fujima student herself. "They were in the dance classes from the time they were small until they were eighteen. It made a difference. You can see it in them. They learned manners. They learned culture. Because Madame Fujima doesn't always speak in English, they learned Japanese words. It was very good for them."

When Madame Fujima makes her annual visits to Japan, the teachers at her old school often encourage her to stay. They tell her that she could be a successful and respected teacher in Japan.

"I won't go. I am happy now. When I first came here it was hard and I was sad. Nobody knew anything. I could only teach the easy dances. The first years were boring. I wanted to have students doing the hard classical dances. Now I'm really happy. Now I have good students who learn the hard dances. It is hard work, lots of traveling. I still like to go back to Japan, but not to stay. America is my home now."

Epilogue: Since 1986, Madame Fujima has traveled to Japan and danced in a special performance in honor of her dancing master there. She continues to teach and travel in Oregon and Washington.

He is buckskin and fringe,
flint and steel, at home
in the library or the wilderness
as he works to divine the secrets
of an ancient way of life.

Minam
Winter

AN OREGON ABORIGINE

"SOMETIMES I'VE CONSIDERED GOING BACK to grad school, wearing my buckskins and carrying all my primitive gear and saying, 'Here I am. I am my master's thesis.'"

Setting aside for the moment the work of tanning his winter's fifty hides, this mountain man — this leathered and fringed vision that looks as if it has sprung from the fur trappers' Rendezvous of 1837, not from an anthropology classroom — bends now to the primeval task of making stone tools. The words come at pauses in the work, falling like the glinting chips and flakes that the hammerstone and the deft hands of Jim Riggs coax off a gleaming shard of obsidian. A blade, surgically sharp and symmetrically formed, is being delivered from the stone, just as it might have a hundred centuries ago. A droplet of blood glimmers on its maker's hand.

"Working stone is a whole complex series of methodologies. It always seems to me that textbook explanations about the types and uses of stone tools don't factor in a learning curve — not over generations but over one lifetime. No one ever allows for the possibility that some historical artifacts are just somebody's mistakes. They exist just because a father looked over a son's shoulder and said, 'That one's not going to work. Better chuck it.'"

Jim Riggs is like that, talking in one breath about academic concerns, such as a complex series of methodologies and in the next about matters more elemental, say, the eating of mice — fur, tails, and all. He is Oregon's aborigine-by-choice, a college-trained anthropologist who lives the primitive life he once studied. In truth, the frontierlike buckskins he favors do not do him justice. A man, after all, has to wear something to get through the cold, icy winters in northeast Oregon's Wallowa County.

But this man's bag of tricks goes back much further than the days of beaver traps and muzzle-loaders — something like twelve thousand years further, to a time when the very earliest Americans had weathered the glacial meltdown of the Pleistocene epoch and had gone on to live the life of hunter-gatherers in the Great

Basin desert of Oregon, Nevada, and Utah. Toss Jim Riggs onto that desert naked and unarmed. Find him again in a week or two, and he will be clothed, sheltered and fed, perhaps a few pounds heavier. Watch him take a dozen students of mixed ages and backgrounds into the sagebrush and the shimmering August heat for a week with only the clothes on their backs, and see them return wishing only that the experience had been longer.

Mention his name in the right circles—to famed Oregon author Jean Auel or to a Hollywood producer or to a growing number of archaeologists and anthropologists—and hear about the multiple dimensions of the soft-spoken writer and artist who lopes through the summers of the Oregon desert country in breechcloth and moccasins.

"Nobody in the United States does what Jim Riggs is doing," says Lucile Housley, director of the Malheur Field Station, the growing academic research center in the middle of the southeast Oregon desert. "Other people teach a few of the things that he does, but nobody has pulled all the hunter-gatherer skills together and lives them like he does. He's not just some guy who's gone native and is out running through the bush. And he doesn't pretend to be a professor in a classroom or an expert archaeologist, although he's good enough that he gets hired for archaeological projects. But he has taken primitive survival skills to a level of understanding unlike anybody else. It's unique. It's a whole mindset and a philosophical approach."

His home, when Riggs is not operating out of a pole-and-brush wickiup beside some desert creek or bunking with the Forest Service on some archaeological survey on the flanks of Hells Canyon, is the drafty, high-ceilinged old Minam School, midway between LaGrande and Enterprise. The tin-roofed building, decades past its last formal class, overflows with an eclectic blend of stone tools, stereo equipment, hand-tanned buckskins, paintings, Indian drums, books, arrow quivers, woodstoves, correspondence, rustic furniture, handwoven baskets, manuscripts, and papoose carriers. Aside from a sleeping loft and a cluttered kitchen, the place is a laboratory with a hundred works always in progress.

Perhaps it is appropriate that Riggs lives in a schoolhouse. At forty-one, he has given his life over to learning and teaching prehistoric skills, to mastering the arts and the technologies of another time, another people. "Back when I was doing archaeology classes at Oregon State, my interests kind of changed," he says. "I burned out on excavations and cataloging artifacts. Sometimes I had the feeling that people who were identifying and analyzing stone tools and other pieces didn't know what they were talking about. I wanted to find out for myself. I wanted to make them and use them. I think that no matter what happened in my life, I would have wound up doing what I'm doing now. But there was a period when a whole series of things happened to propel me into this."

Back in 1963, he had arrived at Oregon State University fresh out of Roseburg High School. His goal then was a degree in zoology. He knew that mathematics was his weakness, so he did the registration table shuffle for three years, putting off the terrors of calculus and trigonometry as long as possible. Meanwhile, several trips he had made to eastern Oregon had spawned an avocational interest in anthropology and archaeology. He and a friend talked with university officials. The result was an increase in the school's offerings of anthropology courses, and,

In an old schoolhouse where the collection of implements ranges from stone tools to stereo gear, Jim Riggs delves ever deeper into understanding the culture and mastering the skills of the Indian people of the Great Basin region. The results show in such projects as a shield made of buckskin tanned by Riggs and an Indian motif painted with colors made from natural pigments.

in 1968, the conferring on Jim Riggs of Oregon State University's very first anthropology degree.

"Anthropology was closest to where my interests were," he says. "But mostly I just wanted to get out of school. Right then, the opportunities weren't great. On the days when the business recruiters came to campus, there were never any tables with 'anthropology companies.'" If there were, Riggs probably would not have applied. It was, after all, an era of change, a time for questioning old ways and old values. Riggs admits to entering a sort of dropout, psychedelic phase at that stage of his life. It left him with an antipathy for the trappings of corporate America, with its security, suburbs, and three-piece suits.

He hung around the Oregon State campus as a graduate student for a term, cataloging some artifacts. Then came the series of serendipitous happenings that lured him out of academia and shaped his future. In the summer of 1969, Odd Bjerke, a Norwegian outdoor survival expert who was touring and teaching in America, hired Riggs as an aide for a survival course he was teaching near Sacramento. On his return to Oregon, Riggs was asked to do some similar wilderness survival sessions for the Portland Zoological Society, and he turned some of his new knowledge into free-lance magazine articles.

And then, at the Douglas County Fair in his hometown, he met Arlington Shaefer. The old-timer, who has since died, was a bona fide, full-time mountain man, a living vestige of the nineteenth century. He lived — well, but not legally — on federal land in southern Oregon's Cascades. "Here's this old man," Riggs recalls. "He's dressed like an Indian. He has bows and arrows and buckskin and stone tools and two huge dugout canoes that he's made himself. I'd just come back from a survival course and here he is with all these primitive tools. He knows how to use them and he's talking about survival, too. Only he's not talking about surviving until you get rescued. He's talking about living that way."

For Riggs, the concept glimmered like a spark struck from flint. For the next three years, living as a squatter in an abandoned cabin he found on public land, he was a pupil to Shaefer and another old mountain man. For part of that time, a woman friend shared his dwelling, but for the entire period Riggs immersed himself in the pursuit of the primitive knowledge. Under the tutelage of the two old-timers, Riggs did postgraduate work in toolmaking and bow-and-arrow hunting and hide tanning and food gathering and dozens of other skills.

Through it all, he worked to meld what he was learning in the wild with what he had been taught in the classroom. The approach is still working, still yielding new insights. "I have a lot of friends who are quite capable in primitive skills and processes," he says. "But they don't have that anthropological matrix or framework. Anthropology taught me where the resources are. Even in that period when I lived in the woods, two miles up a trail from any road, I was going to libraries and back to the university all the time. I'd get interested in a topic like bows and arrows and I'd read everything I could find, from popular books to academic papers. Then I'd try to make it work."

From the woods, Riggs went in 1974 to teach his wilderness survival course at Malheur Field Station, the isolated desert research facility that is operated in southeastern Oregon by a consortium of twenty-three Pacific Northwest colleges and universities. Within two years, Riggs dropped the conventional wilderness

"When you live in the woods, people want to know what you do with all your time," Riggs says. "When you try to explain, you sound like a babbling idot. There is always something to do."

survival course, which incorporated modern implements like compasses and knives. In its place, he began focusing on aboriginal skills. Every year since then he has been back at the Malheur station, expanding the aboriginal skills course into two versions, basic and advanced, and putting more and more students through the classes each year.

In the three-week aboriginal skills session, his students spend two weeks at Malheur learning to gather and prepare desert plants, to tan hides and make rudimentary clothing, to work with stone tools, to use friction drills to make fire. Riggs takes them through the construction of shelters, deadfall traps, and snares from natural materials. Then they head off into the desert for a week. The advanced classes take nothing except perhaps bows and arrows they have made. The beginning classes travel with the comparative luxury of tulle reed sleeping mats, stone knives, and a few seeds and roots they have gathered in advance. The students who go into the desert with Riggs taste coyote and camas. They try rattlesnake stew and roasted crickets and anything that shows up under their deadfall traps.

"I usually try to take about twelve people," Riggs says. "We're essentially trying to replicate a typical aboriginal group of hunter-gatherers, which would have been about that size. People learn to be hungry. Sometimes, when we start out without tools or materials, they have to go without fire the first night. One of the rules is that anything you kill, you eat. So if you build a little deadfall trap and it catches a ground squirrel or a mouse, then that's part of your dinner. The first few years, we skinned and dressed the mice. But that didn't leave much, so now we just cook and eat them whole. People learn about how little it takes to get by. And they find out how little time it takes each day to get the food they need. Sometimes they learn to be hungry. It's not too bad, except when everyone's sitting around the fire talking about things like lemon meringue pie. You learn about the best restaurants in the world on my field trips."

That and much more, the sun-glazed graduates say. Judy Willig, a University of Oregon doctoral candidate in archaeology, counts her 1979 outing with a Riggs class as a pivotal personal experience, one that reshaped her view of her chosen field. "If I had my way, I'd make it a prerequisite for anyone who is heading into a career in archaeology," she says. "So few archaeologists understand the flesh and blood of what they study. It's easy to forget about real, live people when you're studying a bunch of stone flakes. Jim's very knowledgeable about what he does. It may not be perfectly accurate in the sense of duplicating exactly what one tribe or one group did. He's pulled together things from a lot of areas to give a good, generalized feel of that Great Basin life-style. The class really affected me. Whenever I think back on it, I'm grateful I had the chance to do it just before I headed into my doctoral work."

Another Riggs fan is Jean Auel, the Oregon author who has spun off three national bestsellers in her Earth's Children series. The tales in her novels hinge on the life-styles and skills of primitive peoples. She took in a Riggs class just before she wrote *The Valley of Horses*. "Jim is very good at what he does, as good or better than anybody in the country," Auel says. "The course at Malheur was a great experience for me. What I learned shows all through my books."

When Auel's first book, *Clan of the Cave Bear*, was translated into a motion picture, the author insisted that the film's producers use Riggs to ensure accuracy in depicting the work and living conditions of the small band in the story. As a result, Riggs found himself en route to a Vancouver, British Columbia, filming location, wondering what difficulties he would encounter working with a group of eighteen actors.

"I headed up there thinking about Hollywood types, and I wasn't sure what to expect," Riggs recalls. "But it was an excellent experience. The group turned out to be better than many of my Malheur classes. They were totally committed, personally and socially, to becoming the Clan. I wanted to show them how they could look and behave as if they'd been Neanderthals all their lives. We worked with stone tools. We did cordage from plant fibers. We skinned and butchered a calf with primitive tools. And they mastered it all. When the director finally showed up, they started teaching him."

The success of the movie and Auel's books has brought Riggs a small measure of fame, including a network television appearance with the author. But mostly, his life remains the same—a mix of summer teaching, winter research, writing, lecturing, and occasional archaeological jobs. Most of the archaeological work is for the U.S. Forest Service, which customarily does archaeological reconnaissance before the start of logging or road-building projects. His book on hide tanning, said to be the most detailed work on the subject, is now in its second printing. Over the past several winters, he has been plotting a book that will pull together all his working knowledge on aboriginal life-styles.

"A book," he says, "is like a snare or a deadfall. You get it set and you can walk away from it and it's producing for you. Every so often you go to the mailbox and there's a royalty check." A man who can survive off the flora and fauna of the forest or the desert, and who needs only a rundown rented schoolhouse for a home, certainly does not require many of those checks. Riggs manages to live on less than $7,000 a year. He is a sort of Renaissance man in buckskins, earning a few dollars from writing, a few from selling craftwork, a few from paintings or drawings, a few from teaching.

Riggs can easily picture himself living this life for another twenty-five years, although he is working to increase his cash income a bit so that he can buy a homesite somewhere in the Wallowa country. There are some horizons yet to be explored. Sometime soon, he wants to walk the Australian outback with that continent's aborigines.

"I'll always need some time to experiment with processes," he says. "You start looking at some primitive skill and you can't say how long it's going to take to learn it. I have to read. I have to get my materials. And then I have to teach myself to do it. When you live in the woods, people want to know what you do with all your time. When you try to explain, you sound like a babbling idiot. There is always something to do. I never run out."

Epilogue: Since 1986, Jim Riggs has worked on archaeological digs in Hells Canyon and has taught more sessions of his aboriginal skills classes in Oregon's Malheur region. The High Desert Museum in Bend, Oregon, has contracted with him to create sagebrush bark sandals, wild rye mats, a bone flute, snare traps, and other pieces for a walk-through exhibit on the Great Basin Indian culture as it existed before white settlement.

It was not the role he would
have forecast for himself,
this industry forester who wages
lonely battles to save the trees.

Port Orford
Spring

THE MAN WHO CROSSED OVER

B EYOND THE CABLE CAR that flits above the Elk River, beyond the path that winds through the tanbark trees, beyond the footbridge that sways over Anvil Creek is the house where Jim Rogers lives.

It is a piece out of another time, this home where creek meets river. Not a colonial or a Georgian or a Queen Anne. But a period piece nonetheless, from that not-so-long-ago time when the long-haired dropouts from the urban rat races headed to greener places they had never known. In the 1960s, they tucked their structural calling cards, hundreds of them, into the hills of Oregon. Houses like this, gonzo-built bits of organic architecture with log beams and rough siding and strange angles and composting toilets and salvage windows and plank doors. Like so many of the others, this back-to-the-land homestead has its garden and firewood pile and chickens outside, its old furniture and threadbare rug and cast-iron cookstove inside.

For the occasional visitor who honks a car horn from the other side of the Elk, Jim Rogers will come out of the house. He will quiet the dogs, cross the footbridge, walk the path, and throw the gasoline-powered cable car into gear. "I find it mostly kind of boring to go to town," he says. "If I didn't have all this political and environmental stuff going, I'd probably just retreat here. I could stay up here weeks at a time without ever going out."

He seems a period piece, too, this man. After all, the woods are full of aging hippies still living out the Age of Aquarius, still reconciling that odd mix of radical politics and rural escapism. With a patriarchal beard that makes him look as fierce as a rebel at the ramparts and a soft-spoken wilderness rationale that makes him sound as reasonable as Thoreau at Walden Pond, surely this denizen of the forest must be one of them.

But Rogers at forty-six is a latecomer to this life. It almost missed him. Until the middle of the 1970s, he was Jim Rogers, forester and timber manager. Back then, he kept the logs flowing to Western States Plywood in Port Orford. Back

then, he sent the cutting crews out to do their business. Back then, he was the guy who levered the millworkers to sign letters and petitions that would thwart the tree-huggers and the environmentalists.

Flowing twenty feet beneath the pitch and yaw of the cable car, the Elk, in more ways than one, mirrors the man above it. In its upper reaches, as it comes out of the Siskiyou Mountains and heads oceanward, it tumbles through the canyons that Rogers clear-cut. And, lower down, it glides past the wilderness he saved.

Though he never planned it that way, the man who rides the cable car wound up burning his bridges behind him. In the midst of it all, with his prestigious eastern university degree and his carefully mapped career, a new set of convictions marched into his life. He followed where they led. Behind him, on civilization's side of the Elk, is the timber industry where he once worked. And over the river, beyond the house and the garden and the chicken pen, is the Grassy Knob Wilderness, 17,200 acres of pristine coastal old-growth forest that he wrested away from his old colleagues.

A country boy from rural New York, he grew up in another kind of forest, roaming the woods of the Niagara escarpment, just a few misty miles downstream from the falls. More often than not, he chose the woods over other boyhood and school activities. After high school graduation in 1960, he headed off to get a forestry degree at Syracuse University. In that era, campus protestors were railing against Syracuse officials for razing ghetto homes to create parking lots. "In some of those things that happened on campus it would be the foresters and the football players versus the demonstrators," he recalls. "Mostly I just stood on the outside and watched. I was a little sympathetic with some of those causes. But I wasn't part of it, either way."

In his college years he spent a summer on a Forest Service fire lookout tower in Montana. From there, he saw possibilities the East had never shown him. When he graduated in 1964, he and his new wife, Jean, headed for the timber country of the Northwest. He worked for a while for the Weyerhaeuser Company and for the Forest Service in the state of Washington. A government transfer took him to the Siuslaw National Forest near Pacific City, Oregon. Three years later he moved to private industry, accepting a job as forester and timber manager for Western States Plywood. Except for an interruption due to a mill closure, he would hold that position until 1974.

He and his wife and two children settled into a home on the coast. It was a good life, the mix of professional forestry and small-town living he had hoped for. His friends were loggers and millworkers and the handful of other timber managers at neighboring mill operations. Those who knew him might have predicted it was a life he would lead until retirement. But, while he had been singularly unaffected by the political consciousness of the 1960s, the part of it that became the environmental movement caught up with him.

"I was like most foresters—a young person who got into the work because he liked the woods," he says. "You become a career forester. Then you find out your job is to kill the trees. And by then it's the way you're making your living. I was

"I was like most foresters—a young person who got into the work because he liked the woods," says Jim Rogers of his professional career. "Then you find out your job is to kill the trees."

starting to see how fast the timber was going. More damage was happening all the time. There were lots of places that I thought were really beautiful, and I was going in and cruising the timber for cutting. It was starting to bother me a little bit. Only I couldn't think about it too much. My number one concern was to keep those logs going to the mill."

By the early 1970s, Rogers was sporting long hair and testing his emerging environmental consciousness on the veteran foresters who were his closest professional friends. The change was not enough to worry his employers, because he kept the logs flowing steadily from the valleys of the Coast Range Mountains. In fact, Rogers acquired a peculiar sort of credibility at governmental hearings on issues such as timber sales and allowable cuts.

"I'd walk up to the microphone with hair halfway down my back and I'd get all these looks that showed they were sure I was some Sierra Clubber who was going to say they should never cut another tree," he says. "Then I'd start talking about the Forest Service prices on timber or how local mills needed a decent log supply. It was the last thing they expected. And they listened, because it was so bizarre that someone would look like me and be a timber manager. After one meeting, all the industry people were shaking my hand and congratulating me."

But they parted company on the issue of Grassy Knob. In his years on the south coast, Rogers had worked often in the scenic Elk River drainage. Though portions of the upper watershed had been heavily logged, the rugged seventeen hundred acres around Grassy Knob had gone untouched. But its time had come. The Forest Service advanced a plan for logging almost all of it except a bit of stream frontage. State fish and wildlife officials, concerned about fish-spawning habitat, wanted to restrict the cut to thirty percent. With difficulty, Rogers persuaded his company's board of directors to endorse the state plan.

But privately, he began to think the unthinkable. He listened to fisheries biologists who anguished over the possiblity of logging on the Elk. On foot, he spent two days in the Grassy Knob timber. "I realized then that this was the last of it," he says. "As far north as you wanted to go, everything had been logged. But this was virgin wilderness. On the coast, it was really all that was left. And it was about to be finished off."

When he first began talking about creating a wilderness, he told himself that staking out such an extreme position might help promote a compromise of very limited logging of the area. In 1974, his company's mill operation, as well as others in surrounding Curry County, closed down, victims of recession. The battle over Grassy Knob continued. Rogers caught some private consulting and forestry contracts. But as he became more firmly linked to the wilderness question, that work fell off. He let it go willingly and supported himself by winning bids on forestry contract work with the Forest Service.

In the midst of the fight, he sold his home and bought forty-two acres at the edge of the Grassy Knob region, where Anvil Creek meets the Elk. He and Jean built their rough-hewn, angular home there. And then, by pre-agreement, she and the children were gone, off to pursue educations. The separation, though permanent, has never become a divorce. Nine years later, Jean is a Stanford University faculty member. She visits occasionally. She and Jim have jointly financed their children's college educations.

In 1978, in the wake of their departure, Jim Rogers redoubled his efforts on Grassy Knob. Port Orford was sometimes puzzled by his activism. But with the puzzlement came a grudging degree of respect and some allies—commercial and sport fishermen, retirees, tourist-oriented businesses. Rogers, with his collection of strange political bedfellows, led the charge against the industry and local government officials. Heading the pro-logging forces was County Commissioner John Mayea. They met again and again in federal hearings where the testimony ran for hours and a final decision seemed always to be another argument, another appeal, another year away.

More than ten years after the battle began, Grassy Knob became a wilderness in the federal RARE II bill of 1983. "It wasn't exactly like I was the winner and my old friends in the timber industry were the losers," Rogers says. "None of them ever told me they thought I was right. But I had the feeling that some of them weren't fighting me as hard as they could." Like other timber industry sympathizers around Port Orford, Mayea packs a curious sort of respect for Rogers, an environmentalist who is not an intruding carpetbagger come to tell the locals how to run their region.

"I never really understood what changed him, but I think he fought fair," Mayea says. "On Grassy Knob, I thought we could truly have our cake and eat it, too. I thought we could log most of the timber and still protect the fish. We both made our best arguments. And he won. I honestly believe he's sincere in what he does. People with ulterior motives will usually show what they're like if enough time passes. But he's stayed the same way. He's committed to what he believes."

In the house across the river, Jim Rogers lives at the edge of the wilderness. A friend, Carrie Osborne, and her son, Ian, share his home. Rogers' wife and children visit regularly. Rogers continues to make his living off competitive bidding for Forest Service contracts. Many of those contracts are for forestry work that precedes logging. For Rogers, that's not an ethical conflict. He's never taken the position that every tree should be saved.

Still, his wars are not over. These days, he has new battle plans spread on the kitchen table. He wants to halt further logging in the upper area of the Elk drainage, ten thousand acres lying east of the new wilderness. Again, years of hearings and campaigning stretch before him. Around Port Orford, no one is betting against his success.

Epilogue: Lobbying hard since 1988, Jim Rogers has succeeded in getting large sections of the Elk River included in new federal and state scenic rivers legislation. His battles have expanded to include challenging proposed sales in the area that he hopes to see become wilderness.

He came out of Africa to America
and then, in the skies over Oregon,
the unschooled man
from the bush gave wings
to his improbable dream.

Springfield
Winter

THE WARRIOR'S QUEST

Hᴇ ᴡᴀs ᴀ ʙᴏʏ in a dusty village in Kenya when it began, a boy with dreams and certainties as old as his tribe.

He would grow to be a warrior of the legendary Maasai. He would wear his hair braided, sleeked with tallow and red ochre. With his spear, he would stalk the lion. He would own cattle, as all the proud Maasai before him had owned cattle. In time, he would be an elder in his village. But then a new dream found him, a dream that would bring him to a faraway place called Oregon. Even now, when he tells it, the story has the ring of a campfire saga: the Maasai hunter back from the bush, recounting his adventure, recapturing his wonder and excitement at all he has seen, all that has happened to him.

"The dream began in my village. The jumbo jet went over. I heard the thundering and saw the smoke in the sky but I didn't understand. They told me it was an airplane. They said it carried people in the sky and that the people were going to Nairobi. I began to dream that someday I would be the man who flew the plane that took the people to Nairobi."

At home, the Maasai, Wilson Laroi's tribe, still resist civilization. With aloofness, courage, and traditions that have given them a standing of almost mythic proportion among all African tribes, the Maasai still raise warriors and still send them out to kill the lion. But Wilson Laroi is not at home. He is half a world away from Kenya. He tells his story on a wintry day in Oregon, with the sweet smell of strong Kenyan tea floating through his Springfield apartment and the accent of his native land lilting through his English. Standing in the corner is a Maasai spear, the one he used to slay the Cape buffalo, the most dangerous animal in East Africa. A zebra skin decorates the wall. Almost as large on another wall is an aeronautical chart of Kenya. What little space remains is plastered with posters of airliners, jet fighters, the space shuttle.

The warrior from the bush is a pilot now. At twenty-four, he is not yet the man who could fly the plane that takes the people to Nairobi. But he is stalking that quarry, closing on that goal with each passing day, each hour of flying time. He has no doubt.

After all, he is Maasai, a man from a tribe that knows itself as the chosen people. With the pride that would be haughtiness if it were not so understated, he believes. Maasai do not fail. Wilson Laroi has completed work on both his private and commercial pilot licenses. He is close, very close, to his instrument flying rating and his multi-engine license. Ahead of him lies California and the training for his airline transport certificate.

"Wilson has a very good shot at doing what he wants to do," says Mickey Duke, Laroi's teacher and the chief instructor at McKenzie Flying Service in Eugene. "I think his goal's realistic. He understands that it probably will take him a little longer to get where he wants to go. But he's out here every day. He's always working. Learning to fly is a totally new environment for anyone. But it's so much different for Wilson. He comes from a world that is totally non-mechanical. It's amazing to me what he's accomplished already."

Indeed, the whole story of Wilson Laroi, the Maasai who would be a pilot, bristles with improbabilities. He stepped from the comfortable world of tribal tradition into a strange new existence that threatened him and frightened him at every turn. He nourished a single-minded dream that seemed little more than a fantasy until the woman from America, from Oregon, befriended him and under-wrote his education. University towns such as Eugene have been a temporary home to many African students, especially students from the East African nations. Decades of colonialism, of modern education, and — more recently — independent nationhood have delivered thousands of educated young Africans to this country in search of skills and degrees.

But of all the tribes of East Africa, none have resisted education, moderniza-tion, and abandonment of traditional ways more than the half-million Maasai of Kenya and Tanzania. Morompi Ole Ronkei, himself a Maasai and a senior at the University of Oregon, estimates that perhaps only twenty of his tribesmen are in this country. "But we are the few who grew up in cities," he says. "We went to good schools. We learned English. We received a good education. That is not Wilson. He's from the village, the bush."

The village was Kilgoris, in Maasai country, in the far western reaches of Kenya. He grew up there in his family's traditional grass house, where the elders of his tribe cope every day with new laws that shrink the Maasai's territory, protect the game they have hunted for centuries, prohibit the traditional cattle-stealing raids on other tribes. Cattle, indeed, are the root of the Maasai culture. They are bound up in the tribe's religion, a set of beliefs hinged on stories that roughly parallel many of the accounts of the Christian Old Testament. In the Maasai version of the Garden of Eden, before mankind's fall, cattle were a gift from the Creator to the Maasai. Hence, stealing them from other tribes is simply a matter of returning them to their rightful owners.

In today's Africa, with civilization crimping the old ways more and more each year, even the Maasai get some exposure to education. But Wilson's, which ended in his early teens, was conducted primarily in Maasai and Swahili. It left him with only a smattering of English and the thinnest glaze of mathematics. At fourteen, his two lower front teeth were cut from his mouth with a knife, a coming-of-age

"I met people who told me that in America I could learn to fly. In my tribe, the old people told me that if I went to America that I would touch the end of the earth and I would be afraid."

event in the Maasai culture. "If you do not cry, you are given a cow," he says. "If you cry, you get a dog because no one wants a dog. I received the cow."

At sixteen, he was circumcised according to the traditional manhood ritual. The centuries-old ceremony is the cornerstone of the Maasai's complex age-group social system, the signal of entry into the ranks of the morani, the tribe's warriors. At that juncture, Wilson Laroi's life seemed mapped to make him part of the group that faces the task of taking the traditional culture, as best it can, into the twenty-first century. But he took a job at Maasai Mara, the vast wildlife preserve that attracts thousands to Kenya each year. With his sharp Maasai eyes and his tracker's instincts, he guided tourists and improved his English a bit.

"I met people who told me that in America I could be educated and learn to fly," he says. "But I did not know how to go. I did not know where was America. In my tribe, the old people told me that if I went to America that I would touch the end of the earth and that I would be afraid. They told me that it was bad. They said I would be a slave."

One of the visitors to Maasai Mara was Cindy Avila. From her horse ranch outside of Eugene she was on her first trip to Africa. Wilson was eighteen when he met the woman from America. Avila, who now lives full-time in Kenya, is modestly wealthy. The Dee Bar Ranch, the quarter-horse breeding operation that she and her former husband operated for years, garnered an international reputation. Animals worth hundreds of thousands of dollars were bred and sold from the Dee Bar. Avila was easing out of the operation, which she would eventually sell, when she met the soft-spoken Maasai guide in the Kenyan bush.

"All my life, in business and in work, I have been lucky," she says. "It seemed like everything I touched turned out very well. I came to Africa and I saw the lack of opportunity and the hardships which people suffered, and how they suffered it with such good heart. Somehow, I thought it was time for me to put back into the world some of the things I'd taken out. Then I met Wilson. There is something very, very exceptional about Wilson. Other people who meet him see it, too. To this day, I can't describe it in words. But it's there. He's proved it with what he's already accomplished."

No grand plan to make Laroi a pilot came from that first meeting. Avila returned home after promising the young Kenyan she would bring him to the United States and launch the basic educational work needed before he could pursue any career. But getting out of Africa was Wilson's job. Alone, he had to find his way to the modern city of Nairobi, to penetrate the bureaucracy of Kenya and America, to learn of physical examinations and passports and airline tickets. The lion and the leopard never struck such fear in him as did the elevator and the escalator.

"I did not have anybody to help me do this thing," he says. "I had to do it on my own. I went to Nairobi. Alone. I was the boy from the bush in the city. It was all strange, like another planet. There were all of these paper things I did not know. I would go back and forth from my village to Nairobi. I learned by myself to stay in hotels and take taxi cabs. It took me three months to get a passport. One guy would tell me, 'No.' But I would go on. I would not accept it. I am a Maasai. People do not tell me 'No.'"

Sometimes, the warrior admits, he cried. He was robbed on a street in Nairobi, his clothing and money stolen. With no chance to return home and say farewell to his parents, he boarded the plane for America on a day early in 1982. When the 747 lifted from the earth, he thought he had died.

Avila met him in Los Angeles. Deliberately, she plunged him into a series of new experiences, from scuba diving in the Caribbean to gambling in Las Vegas to wintering at the Montana home of her parents. "Mostly, I wanted to get him some education, so that he could develop his English," Avila says. "I knew that the thing about flying was there with him. But it was such a faraway, fingertips kind of dream, the way you or I might talk about flying to the moon. We had other things to take care of first."

Wilson spent a year at a community college in Arizona, improving his English and reading skills. In Wyoming, he did some training as a veterinary technician, acquiring skills that might serve his people's cattle-based economy. Then came the University of Oregon's program for students who were pursuing English as a second language. On free weekends, he sometimes traveled in a small plane with Warren Harper, a Junction City farmer and pilot who befriended him.

"After a year or so at the university, I think Wilson and I both sensed that he was kind of drifting and not certain where he was heading," Avila says. "So I sat him down and we had a real heart-to-heart. It was flying that he wanted. But he was afraid. It wasn't physical fear. It was like he was afraid that he would take my money and not be able to do it. I told him that what I wanted him to learn most of all in the United States was that it's not a problem to try and fail. It's only a problem if you don't try at all. And that's how we started."

The rest is history. It is in the license that hangs in the same apartment with the skins of animals and the Maasai spear. It is in the flying hours that mount steadily in his logbook. It is in the way he slides behind the controls and wings off into a gray Oregon sky on his own. "I always will remember the first day I soloed," he says. "There is a wonderful freedom in flying. Just you and the machine. You hear it and feel it. You see the birds fly beneath you. It's beautiful."

Still, the most difficult stretch of the path he has set for himself lies ahead. Mickey Duke, the flying instructor, talks about how simple experiences like playing with a toy truck or changing the batteries in a flashlight are part of the lifetime reservoir of mechanical experiences that an American youth accumulates and brings to the task of learning to fly. Wilson started his reservoir only six years ago. It is still under construction. More years of work lie ahead for him, time in which his life will be devoted solely to flying lessons and studying. In Nairobi, his patron will continue writing the checks to cover the considerable expenses of his training and his living.

"I've never had a day of regret since I started this," Avila says. "When you look at everything Wilson's had to overcome, barriers of language and education and sociology and race, what he's achieved is amazing. In his own sweet, kind, gentle way, Wilson is making this work."

Wilson Laroi wants only to complete his training and take it home to Kenya. He sees multiple possibilities. He might be a flight instructor or a pilot for one of the missionary operations that serve the bush. Or he might find a place with Kenya Airways. Though it would take years of building his hours and upgrading his certification to ever-larger aircraft, he might indeed become the man who flies the plane that carries to the people to Nairobi. If it happens, he will take his Oregon memories into African skies, aware that experience has changed him and that he will always be a man with a foot in two cultures.

"I came to America to be educated and to be a pilot," he says. "I will go back home wearing a suit. But I will not give up my tribe. I want my people to stay the way they are. I would not want to change them. And I would not change myself. Inside, I am still Maasai. I want always to be a Maasai person."

Epilogue: Since 1987, Wilson Laroi has obtained his instrument rating and his multi-engine license, and has completed additional training in San Diego, California. He has married Carolee Hamilton, the daughter of Medford, Oregon, missionaries who work in Kenya. Cindy Avila pursues the traveler's life and has lived recently in Thailand and the Maldive Islands. Pat Hadnagy of San Diego has begun work on a documentary film about Wilson Laroi's improbable odyssey, with some of the filming to be done in Kenya. In the spring of 1989, Wilson and his wife returned to Africa, so that he could take Kenyan licensing tests and begin a flying job. He has begun to talk of creating his own charter flight company. He would call it Air Maasai.

Daily he wrestles the dilemma:
will it be an intellectual life
in academia or the delight
of watching quicksilver dogs
race across green pastures?

Philomath
Spring

A MATTER OF CHOICE

H<small>E SUSPECTS HE IS OUT OF PLACE</small> in both his worlds. And the oft-postponed task of choosing between them looms large indeed. Rob Lewis, the Ph.D. candidate, the American who slipped off to live among Scotland's shepherds, the man who sees poetry when a dog waltzes a band of sheep across a green Oregon hillside, never expected it to come to this. But here he is, at thirty-two, with years of his life and thousands of dollars invested in an education, wondering if he will wind up trading off academia for the quicksilver dogs that bring him so much joy.

At Oregon State University, his doctoral adviser is occasionally impatient with the bright student who is behind on his work because of time stolen to devote to the ancient task of training sheep dogs. On the courses where Oregon's sheep raisers meet to find out whose dog is best, it is another story. Among the stockmen, reservations have ebbed to acceptance of this intellectual Easterner — a non-farmer at that — who defeats them as often as not.

So which way will Lewis go? Perhaps worse than the curse of potential is the curse of two gifts. If he were, say, a researcher who also showed promise as a surgeon, the world might respect either choice. But this choice seems different.

"I don't know," he says. "I ask myself every day. Here I am. I'm a highly educated person. The world tells you that you should use your talents. I've had all these scholarships and assistantships and degrees. Society has invested all this money in me. I'm supposed to be thinking about paying it back. And then there's the dogs. I don't even know how to explain about the dogs. I love the dogs themselves. When I work with them, there's just this wonderful feeling. Whenever I come back from being out with them, I feel rejuvenated."

He is the son of a white-collar family from eastern Virginia. They were parents of high expectations. He was a student of solid promise. After high school he was off to prestigious Duke University. A career in medicine or business was likely. But restlessness overtook him. In 1975, at the age of twenty, he headed for Europe. Toward the end of his tour he found the Isle of Skye, one of the Hebrides

Islands in the North Atlantic at the east edge of Scotland. The isle is a rugged place, with rocky coasts and heathered hills. Since the Middle Ages it has been home to clans of sheep-raising Scots. They still walk the hills with shepherd's crooks and, with their famed border collies, run their flocks on unfenced land.

On a summer's day, Lewis hiked off across some of that land. His life was about to change. "I know it sounds very romantic but I was walking and I found these two pups," he says. "I knew they must belong to someone, so I started looking." The first door on which he knocked was opened by Malcolm MacLeod, descendant of an ancient clan. He was the dogs' owner. Over the next two days, he introduced Lewis to a world where the link between man and dog is the stuff of legend, where border collies get credit for near-human intelligence, where the lore says a dog may die of heartbreak if its master passes away.

"I don't remember clearly everything I saw the day he took me out," Lewis says. "But what I did see was an incredible connection between man and dog, without any animosity or force by Malcolm. It was like a choreographed event, almost too much to believe."

Lewis left for America with one of MacLeod's collie pups. He knew nothing of training dogs for sheep work. But the dog was quick and bright, so Lewis taught her tricks as he wrapped up his bachelor's degree in math and economics. But clearly, career goals had changed. He took a junior high school teaching job. During that year, his dog was killed by a car. In the spring, Lewis resigned and returned to Europe. He showed up at MacLeod's door again. This time he stayed, hiring on to work with one of MacLeod's sheepman neighbors. Among the taciturn Scotsmen, who willingly showed him much but explained nothing, he sought to unravel the mystery of the dogs. MacLeod was his mentor. But that only meant that Lewis could watch whenever he wished.

Often he was frustrated, uncertain whether he was even welcome. His failures were frequent. Once, working an unresponsive dog under MacLeod's eye, he let frustration and discouragement surface. And he learned a lesson. "When he saw that, Malcolm just berated me," he says. "He was shaking his shepherd's crook at me. He read me out in English and then in Gaelic. He told me I had to decide for myself whether I was going to do this thing or not. It was probably the most important lesson of my life."

Later, Lewis decided to enter a dog he had trained in two trials. Some of the Scots snickered at the idea. The first trial was a fiasco. But in the second, against some of the best dogs and handlers in the world, Lewis and the dog placed third. Even the skeptics congratulated him.

By 1979, he was back in the United States with another dog, a female named Lass. He taught for two years and wrapped up a master's degree in education. But the idea of doing something with his dog and with his skills was always there. He headed west. Over the next three years, he struck a compromise between avocation and academia by making Lass a working sheep dog and by completing another master's, this time in animal science, at Montana State University in Bozeman. He met his wife, Sarah, there. During his time at the university, he ran a small flock of sheep on rented property.

The two-pronged life-style was pleasant and, as always, Lewis did well in his studies. But the combination seemed only to defer a decision. In 1984, he won an assistantship and entry to the doctoral program at Oregon State University. He admits a pivotal factor in the decision was his eagerness to live in a state with one of the nation's most active circuits of sheep dog trials. The Oregon competitors are no slouches. The best of them have made their own trips to Scotland, and compete with dogs they have acquired there. But none of the Oregonians had spent the amount of time there that Lewis had. For a year or more, they did not know what to make of the scholarly newcomer.

Out on the course, where a handler must stand in position and have his dog move a group of sheep through complex maneuvers with a minimum of voice commands or whistles, Lewis showed what he could do. "He won a lot," says Virgil Brown of Scio, one of the state's top competitors. "I called him a schoolboy and at first I thought it was just schoolboy luck. But I watched him for a while and I changed my mind. He's good. He's had some real tutoring."

In Oregon, Lewis acquired more dogs. He frequently trains dogs, as well as their owners, for ranching operations. He is now an accepted fixture on the competition circuit and, with Scio's John Carter, is acknowledged as one of Oregon's top two handlers. As always, he has done well in academia. His doctoral work gets good reviews. But it comes slowly. Dogs and competition vie for his time. Lewis is almost certain he will be a bit late on the looming deadline for completion of his work.

The academic track Lewis is on could be expected to route him into a life of teaching and research. His mentor is Howard Meyer, an Oregon State professor of animal science. Meyer knows Lewis as a student of high promise, a man who could make a strong contribution to academic agriculture. But he is not certain it will happen. More than once, he has suggested that his student spend less time with dogs and more with books. "I have no concern about his intellectual ability at all," Meyer says. "But I think Rob looks at the academic world and isn't entirely certain he wants to get into it. We all have peripheral interests. But for most of us they don't take over."

Lewis sees the conflict, too. He is a man who seems inclined to view every decision, every choice, as a moral one. In 1986, he had accumulated some savings to take himself and Sarah to Scotland. He pondered, and then put the money into bringing Malcolm MacLeod to Oregon, to see the dogs descended from Scottish border collies do their work in America. But, compared to decisions about his own future, that choice was easy. With the end of his academic work nearing, Lewis will not predict what he will be doing five years from now. Might he take his Ph.D., bid farewell to academia, and head off to work sheep and dogs?

"I have no solution. I know that sometime I'm going to have to choose between a career in the academic world and something like being just a sheep farmer who is good with dogs. I think about it all the time. And it's always a dilemma."

Epilogue: Rob Lewis has completed his doctorate. In 1989, he contracted to work on an Alaskan research program, where his dog would be used to herd and gather game birds for banding during their non-flying molt period. Lewis continues to explore such options for combining his academic background and dog-handling skills.

IS THERE
LIFE AFTER
DEATH?

TRESPASS
HERE AND
FIND OUT

"I should've got married again,
but I never did.
A railroader's a dry land sailor.
It's not the life for a married man."

Mapleton
Summer

THE OLD MAN OF THE RIVER

Aʜ, ʙᴜᴛ ᴛʜᴇ ᴍᴇᴍᴏʀɪᴇs are good. Hard work and hard times, stagecoaches and mailboats, boarding house teachers and itinerant timber fallers, even moonshine and murder. Seldom any coin in the pocket but almost always venison on the table. Like an aging king in some shabby court, Charlton Richardson at seventy-three plays it all back for the visitors who never seem to stop wandering through the door of his shanty of a house off the highway between Walton and Mapleton.

"I have so much company that some days I don't have any time to do anything but talk to people," he growls. "I can't remember a day when somebody didn't stop in. Some days it's standing room only in here. State cops and timber buyers a lot of the time. People with car trouble and people who just stop to talk. I've had ten or fifteen of 'em in here at a time."

Even for native Oregonians, it is easy to forget how isolated and frontierish the deep and timbered valleys of the Coast Range were until nearly the midpoint of the twentieth century. Well up into the 1930s, a trip to the beaches of the coast from inland points such as Eugene or Salem could be a two-day adventure, and one not to be tackled in winter. Old-timers who grew up without electricity are common enough in the Oregon of the 1980s. But Richardson, a third-generation child of the Siuslaw Valley, rode a stagecoach to school in the 1920s. When he was born in 1913 at a doctor's office downriver in Florence, the only way home was a mailboat that hauled him and his parents—along with flour, hardware, and milk cans—up the Siuslaw River to Mapleton.

"He's the old man of the river," says Phil George, a state trooper and a frequent visitor at the shanty by the Siuslaw. "I just love the old man, and all kinds of other people do, too. I don't know if I could handle his life-style, but the things he knows are amazing. Anytime I've got a question about a family name or a road I've never heard of, he's the guy I see."

Colorful history it is that Richardson delivers. And some of it includes his own milestones. It is, for example, a point of roguish pride with him that, in his

---

sometimes misspent youth, he was the first poacher ever arrested by the first game officer ever sent to the Siuslaw Valley.

"The law was a long time getting in here," he says. "I remember seeing guys with their ears bit off in the logging camps. I've got a lump on my lip. I walked right into a fist one night. After that, every time I started thinking about getting into a fight I'd rub that lump and wonder if I really wanted another one. It was rough like that—farmers and homesteaders like my folks on one side of the river, and the moonshiners worked on the other side. There was always killings around the moonshiners. There's a deep hole down in the river where they'd tie a weight on a body and throw it in. There was lots more down there in that hole for company. The law never knew."

For all the tale-spinning, Richardson lives as much in the present as in the past. Not for him the role of the rheumy-eyed oldster who can only talk about living. The man in the patched-together house beside the Siuslaw still has plenty of it to do himself. Lean, energetic and quick of step, with a mustache that curves to his chin and brown eyes that glint when there is a story to be told, he roams the Siuslaw hills with gun and dog. He fishes, gardens, splits wood, and—on occasion—fires up his ancient bulldozer for a bit of work.

It may be the visitors who keep him young. From fishing parties to delegations of public officials to motorcycle gangs, they show up regularly on his porch. "Is there life after death? Trespass here and find out," is the tough message carried on the door, which inevitably swings open to reveal a welcoming grin.

Inside, the place is an improbable combination of home, museum, and work-shop. Bachelor quarters, unquestionably, with an umbra of stovetop splatters climbing one wall and barely a square foot of work surface visible on the cluttered kitchen countertop. At one end of the living room-kitchen is the ancient overstuffed chair with a well-worn deerhide hanging over one arm, where he receives visitors and holds court. Close at hand are the telephone and a citizens band radio. Years of phone numbers are jotted on the front of painted wooden cabinets. A gas lantern swings overhead, at the ready for the next power outage.

The collection of a lifetime of wheeling and dealing and bartering festoons the place. Old hats and fishing rods, bouquets of keys and a plastic grenade hang from the ceiling. Around the room are traps, a beaded pillow, a bearskin, a nineteenth-century collar box, Jack Daniel's bottles, the instrument kit of some pioneer surgeon, framed photographs of homesteading ancestors. Hung from the fireplace are the puttee leggings Richards wore in the National Guard in the years before World War II. On the kitchen table is a vast assortment of miscellaneous hardware. "I keep it there because the company likes to go through it," Richardson says. "Gives them something to talk about."

In spite of all his deep-rooted historical connections with the Siuslaw country, Richardson is not a lifetime resident. He grew to manhood on the river in a family home where teachers, loggers, and timber buyers often were taken in as boarders. He was the lone graduate of the Class of 1932 in long-gone Siuslaw High School. Then came a few years of odd-jobbing—splitting firewood, putting up hay, logging, peeling cascara bark for the pharmaceutical industry. He worked on government survey crews, too, an experience that only served to expand his knowledge of the hills and hollows of western Oregon.

There was a marriage that lasted nine years or so and produced two children. In those years he moved out of the valley, landed a job with the Southern Pacific Railroad, and wound up working three decades as a brakeman and conductor. He acquired property in west Eugene and, with his father, operated a saw filing shop. Sometimes he tended two jobs at once, filing saws in railroad cabooses out on the mainline. "I did a lot of drinking in those years," he says. "It was all lovin' whiskey, not fightin' whiskey. I should've got married again but I never did. A railroader's a dry-land sailor. It's not the life for a married man."

He retired from the railroad in 1969 and spent a few years bar-hopping and card-playing in Eugene. Then, in 1973, he took what he describes as his life's last taste of liquor and headed back to the Siuslaw, back to a piece of the old family holdings. He has been established there ever since, comfortable in his role as the river's resident character. His home, patched with tin and tarpaper, and packed with the effluvia of a lifetime, stands on a small piece of ground below Highway 126 and above the Siuslaw.

Out on the long stretch of road that runs beside the river, the weatherworn house has become a sort of oasis, the place where accident victims and drivers with car trouble often show up in time of need. Flares and flashlights are always ready by the door. Police officers who work the highway have their own stories about Richardson heading into the night and taking charge until the red lights of emergency vehicles arrive.

"This is just the kind of place people look at and think they can use a phone or borrow a gallon of gas," Richardson says. "Happens all the time. I've had them bleeding and dyin' here, too. Sometimes two or three of them from accidents up on the road, with me trying to patch 'em up and keep 'em going until the ambulance gets here."

Between his railroad pension and some investment income, Richardson lives comfortably. His surroundings and the tiny old house are a matter of preference, not necessity. "Some people only want a good balance in their checkbook or a few bonds. I've got some of that. But that's not important. What's important is bein' able to raise a garden or shoot a deer. I trade all the time. Somebody has something they don't want, I'd deal with 'em. I'll get took or I'll take. It doesn't matter much which it is. Money don't mean that much to me. I have everything I want. Aren't lives amazing the way they work out?"

Epilogue: Along the Siuslaw, life goes on. In the winter of 1988, at seventy-five, Charlton Richardson took his hounds to the hills and bagged two bears.

With thin financial resources
and strong moral commitment,
Alan Kapuler would save
the world's stock
of green and growing things.

Corvallis
Spring

Doctor Garden

Orchids and baseball.

It began with that unlikely pairing of youthful avocations in the shadow of Ebbetts Field back in Brooklyn. Latin genus names and bubblegum trading cards. Cypripedium on the stem in the morning and Gil Hodges at bat in the afternoon. All the way, life has been a stew of contrasts for Alan Kapuler. On the one hand, there was Kapuler the over achiever, Ph.D. biologist, and one-time cancer researcher. On the other, there is Kapuler at forty-five, the man who marched out of academia and found a task he considers more important. And it is . . . gardening.

Granted, it is not every day that Yale honor graduates are found spending their prime earning years puttering in the soil and happily knocking down $18,000 a year. But Kapuler is a gardener who plants with a sense of mission. This gardener talks — unceasingly, scientifically and, most of all, eloquently — about saving the world, or at least the gene pool of its plants. "I'm trying to move gardening to another level," he says. "I'm trying to show that gardening is not trivial. We have a whole planetary history to take care of. But we're ensuring the extinction of half the world's flora by paying no attention to the biological issues we face."

Historically, the world reserves special treatment for those who would save it. It may martyr, physically or politically, the few it takes seriously, and dish up head-shaking, temple-tapping skepticism to the rest. But Kapuler has long since come to terms with how the world looks at him.

Those who knew him in his days as a young scientist predicted a promising research career. But some of them, like Professor Howard Temin, a cancer researcher and Nobel Prize winner at the University of Wisconsin, saw a bit of unrest in the bright young researcher. "That was in the '60s," Temin says. "Alan was typical of what one thinks of as a young person in the '60s, more so than many other graduate students and young scientists. He was a smart person and a competent scientist. But he had already done some traveling and other things that gave him an outlook different than other scientists his age."

The son of a high-achieving Brooklyn Jewish family — his father was a psychiatrist and his mother an artist — Kapuler was on an academic fast track from early childhood. At age eleven, he landed a part-time job at the prestigious Brooklyn Botanical Gardens. He memorized Latin names for two thousand plants and learned grafting and other horticultural techniques.

Still, he was something less than an academic grind. He spent hours at sandlot baseball, amassed baseball cards by the hundreds, and — autograph pen in hand — haunted the player entrance at the Brooklyn Dodgers' stadium. "Ebbetts Field was right next to the Brooklyn Botanical Gardens," he says. "My two loves were side by side. You could get in free for the last three innings of any game, so I could hang out with the orchids and then go see the Dodgers. It was a routine."

Despite such diversions he won a national science award in high school. He entered Yale at sixteen, just as the field of molecular biology was opening up. Fascinated, he majored in biology and graduated with honors at twenty. Next was Rockefeller University where he earned a doctorate in medical biochemistry. Then came a faculty position at the University of Connecticut. Kapuler established a microbiology department there and embarked on research work with cancer and respiratory viruses. By most standards, he had arrived. He was not convinced.

"The peace movement was rising," he says. "Long hair was growing. Dylan was singing. It was a time when you could really feel good about being alive. I saw a lot of things in academia I didn't like. I started feeling that I just didn't want to be stuck as some kind of junior officer in the university education business. It was time for me to find my life."

In 1971, the twenty-nine-year-old professor resigned. And he headed west. He bounced along the coast, then settled on a commune near Jacksonville in southern Oregon. Over the next decade he met Linda Sylvester, who is now his wife, and he discovered gardening. He was fascinated. Gardening and the expansive idea of preserving the world's seed heritage came to dominate his life.

With Sylvester and a friend, Alan Venet, he launched a small business based on harvesting and marketing the seeds of rare and threatened plants. Early on, the business made only a few hundred dollars a year. "For several years I lived on about $50 a month," Alan says. "I was living on someone else's farm. I grew my food. So $50 went a long way. Among the people I lived with, I was always the poorest one, the one with the highest credentials, the most income potential, and the least money." In the early 1980s, Kapuler and Sylvester left southern Oregon and gradually developed the business. Now called Peace Seeds, it provides a modest income. They are aided by some of Oregon's large organic farmers, who believe in the work and provide tilled ground for test plots.

These days, Kapuler works at raising both seeds and consciousness. He wants people to think about seeds or, more correctly, about the planet's gene pool. He is not alone in his concern. Over the past decade, scientists have sounded alarms over the pace of plant extinction. They point to slash-and-burn agriculture in tropical areas, urbanization, pollution, and logging as factors that are pushing two species a day into extinction. They are increasingly worried about the effects of hybridization and overbreeding on food plants.

The world's staple food supply depends on about two dozen plant species. Researchers say that the ancestral varieties of those plants, which fed humans for centuries, had extremely high resistance to disease. Scores of those varieties are dying out or have already been lost because of the attention focused on newer varieties. Many plant scientists believe saving old food plant varieties is crucial. They fear that new ones may be genetic time bombs, with hidden vulnerability to disease or environmental change. "The good heirloom seeds that we still have exist simply because they were nutritious and healthful," Kapuler says. "Every one of the worthwhile plants that's been around for a hundred or more generations is around because it worked. It grew, it didn't die and it fed the kids."

With a seed stash that includes a 1500-year-old strain of beans discovered at a New Mexico archaeological site and heirloom plant varieties from descendants of U.S. pioneer families, Kapuler is doing something about saving threatened strains of wild and cultivated plants. Typically, he obtains a handful of such seeds and then produces marketable quantities for people interested in preserving threatened plants. Others do similar work. Seed-exchange cooperatives have gotten into the act. Researchers and governments are there also.

But Kapuler calls most seed-saving work piecemeal and unsystematic, as futile as launching lifeboats in a typhoon. The dropout scientist is forging what he thinks will be a master plan for saving the planetary gene pool. At its heart is a complex system that Kapuler sees as a roadmap to plant preservation. In elaborate charts and lengthy stream-of-consciousness writings, he outlines ways to track hundreds of plants — both cultivated and wild — back to their genetic forebears.

"Up to now, there have been a lot of people concerned about the plant gene pool but no systematic way to know what to preserve," he says. "I've created a system that will allow us actually to know which plants are crucial to save." As a small part of that work, for example, he has proposed an Oregon garden focusing on a fruit like the apple and displaying, in order, all the strains that preceded varieties such as the Granny Smith or Red Delicious. Multiply that project a thousandfold, extend it to nearly extinct strains of food plants and to vanishing jungle plants. Stir in laboratory nutritional analysis of heirloom garden plants. Scour the earth for threatened plants. Consider all of those things, and the scope of Kapuler's ideas begins to emerge.

As a scientist, he believes in his work, talks about it with the zeal of a tent revival evangelist. But enough native Brooklyn humor remains for him to see that the packed seed room in his small home is an unlikely launching pad for his monumental mission. Kapuler is stalking some grants that would let him get on with the research necessary to advance his work. And he has considered the idea that it might be easier to make his peace with academia and regain a platform for his views. But that is not likely to happen.

"I'm not sure academia would want me at all," he says. "I'm radical on several levels. I wouldn't want to spend my time teaching a bunch of kids the same repetitive programmed behavior that's been taught for years, not when what we need is some really original research. It isn't easy doing it this way. But I see beautiful things disappearing every day. I'm a biologist. Somebody has to be willing to do this work. I have no choice."

Epilogue: The work of Peace Seeds goes on, although its profitability has not greatly increased. Since 1988, gardening publications have begun to take note of Alan Kapuler's work, and occasional speaking engagements come his way.

Pleasure may often be mere happenstance,
but for many who live in Oregon it is
a matter of clear and considered choice.

FAST DOGS AND WHIMSICAL LADIES

No, you never get any fun
Out of the things you haven't done.
— OGDEN NASH

WHAT WE DO WITH THE TIME we call our own may say more about us than all the hours and all the years we spend in earnest pursuit of livelihood.

I have yet to touch each of the ways that the people of Oregon have fun, though it seems a noble goal. The annual Imnaha Bear Meat Barbecue and Rattlesnake Fry, to name just one, remains on my list of stories yet to be written. But each time I check something off that list, or stumble upon a heretofore unsuspected Oregon diversion, my understanding of the personality of the state grows a bit.

Much of this Oregon fun is public, though not ostentatious. I will take this precious time I can call my own, say men in a coastal logging town, and I will spend it at the unique tavern where my father, and his father before him, bellied up to the bar. And much of it is private: I will take this time, says a cowboy on the opposite side of the state, and I will use it to write about the men and women who settled and worked this land before me.

Among them all, the people with years to call their own may be the most innovative users of that time. Oregon is a haven, I am convinced, for that peculiar brand of retiree — a misnomer if ever there was one — who thinks that rocking chairs make good firewood. How else to explain a man in his seventies, laughingly risking his neck as he races his streaking greyhounds across farm fields and river bottomland? Or a pair of delightfully whimsical women who, with successful careers behind them, construct a dream home, at once bizarre and perfect, overlooking the waters of Coos Bay?

Once I stood at a roadside with a much-traveled man who had settled here late in life. "Oregon has more people doing crazy things than any place I've ever lived," he told me. Apparently, he was proudly including himself.

"No stray women. No fights.
No trouble. The troublemakers don't
come here. Those older gentlemen
in the back, they're the
real bosses of this place."

Coquille
Summer

THE WAY IT USED TO BE

SUDDENLY IT IS 1938, going on 1918.

Like flies locked forever in amber, Dempsey and Tunney and Firpo are caught in their classic gloves-up stances in ancient framed photographs on the wall of Bill's Place. In another of the pictures on the much-bedecked walls, young Jimmy Agostino, a smartly dressed nineteen-year-old, poses against the bar on a day in 1927. And, over there, just across the room, a real-life Agostino at seventy-six deals yet another hand of pinochle to his cronies.

Belly up to the bar. Hang a foot over the brass rail. You'll have to stand. There are no stools at Bill's. No women either. And that's no accident.

Just for a moment, block out incidentals like the microwave and the television. Suddenly you're standing in an old-fashioned men's bar, the kind of tavern that, decades ago, was a fixture in working-class towns all over Oregon, all over America. They're mostly gone now. Their successors run to plastic ferns and chrome-legged stools and Naugahyde booths and cigarette machines and under-sized pool tables with damnable coin slots and juke boxes that drown honest conversation. Women, too.

But not Bill's. Time and the sort of progress that works to homogenize America have passed it by. And somehow, in a world of liberated femininity, it survives with the blessings of Coquille's women. The spittoons are polished and functional. The wood floors are oiled, the way wood floors were half a century ago. The cigar case is well-stocked. The walnut and maple scoring beads are neatly on wires above the pool tables. Loggers and mill workers swap lies at the same standup bar where their fathers and grandfathers once stood. In the back of the cavernous room, old men count trump and slap pinochle cards on rough tables with four-by-four legs, linoleum tops and hubcap ashtrays.

"My dad and grandad drank beer here," says Ken Wilson, a Coquille logger. "It's a good old bar, mainly because nobody's old lady is threatened by them drinking here. It's not that kind of place. No stray women. No fights. No trouble.

The troublemakers don't come here. Those older gentlemen in the back, they're the real bosses of this place. They get a lot of respect. The rest of us wouldn't tolerate anybody coming in here and doing anything to make them uncomfortable."

Coquille Police Chief Corky Daniels agrees. "It's a different kind of bar," he says. "Very old-fashioned. I can't remember the last time we had a call there."

Those old guys at the card table were young guys indeed back in 1918, when Felix Machon, a Coquille entrepreneur, started construction of a small downtown hotel. He opened it with the bottom floor housing a restaurant and a bar. The paint was barely dry when Prohibition arrived in 1920. The bar, like so many others in those times, limped through the dry years as a cigar store and pool hall. Like Agostino, many of the longtime customers frequented the place back then as high school students. By 1928, the building was owned by Bill Fortier, a legendary figure in Coquille history. He made the place headquarters for the Coquille Loggers, a successful semi-professional baseball team that barnstormed Oregon and assured that Bill's Place would forever be a haven for the male sports fans of southern Coos County.

Over those same years, various businesses shared the first floor with Fortier's operation. "The whole building was always a gathering point," says seventy-nine-year-old Harold Simmons, who found Bill's after he landed on the coast aboard a tramp steamer in 1921. "At one time part of the building was a hiring hall. A guy ran an office here and hired for all the lumber companies. I hired out of it myself once and went to washing dishes in a lumber camp."

The taps opened again at Bill's Place when Prohibition was repealed in 1933. Never mind that it was the Depression. Business at the bar was good. Some nights the loggers and mill hands ringed all three pool tables and stood six-deep at the bar, backed up against the long magazine rack on the opposite wall. In 1938, Fortier stretched the bar by nine feet and knocked out a wall to accommodate two more pool tables. Except for the ever-growing collection of sports photographs, hunting trophies and backbar memorabilia donated by customers, Bill's has seen no significant changes in decor since then.

Fortier sold the operation in 1953. In 1974, it came up for sale again and Burt Fry, then a Coquille insurance man, decided it was time to switch businesses. "I'd told Dean Caudle, the owner, that if he ever decided to sell, I wanted a chance at it. It was just this bar that interested me. I never would have considered another one. When he gave me the chance to buy it, I talked it over with my wife. She said I might as well go ahead and get it—I was there all the time anyhow." Fry, a successful touring jazz musician before settling into the insurance business, changed nothing. Despite his musical background, he wouldn't even consider a juke box. The only concession to modern communications is television, which, except for the occasional presidential assassination attempt or Libyan bombing excursion, is always tuned to a sports event. The photographic generations of Coquille Loggers peering down from the walls would understand.

For the last forty-eight years, the bar has occupied the entire first floor of the old hotel, except for a small storefront space that's been a barber shop for decades. Upstairs, Fry still runs ten sleeping rooms, with a bathroom down the hall. The tenants, all men, tend to stay a long time. When the weight of their years gets too heavy, Fry helps them relocate to nursing homes.

The magazine rack at Bill's is a bit smaller these days. And it runs more to fleshly delights than to the hunting and sports publications that filled it in the bar's early years. But even now, a few well-thumbed *National Geographics* share the shelves. "The magazines was always a big thing here years ago," says Simmons, with an old man's smile. "But no magazines like the ones now. If they'd had those fifty years ago, the Methodists would have been right down here in no time."

Bill's is still basically the men-only bar that Agostino and Simmons remember from their youth. A month or more can pass without a woman taking a drink at the bar. But the past few years have seen a growing number of Coquille women, often wives or sweethearts of regular customers, making the just-once foray to see what the place is like. "Yeah, a woman comes in now and then," a logger says. "It stops the conversation every time. But nobody's rude. Most of the time it's just sort of the reverse of women's day at a country club. Men could probably go out and play golf on that day. But most of them are considerate enough to stay away. And that's the way most of the women in town are with Bill's."

The Coquille woman who may see the most of Bill's is Debbi Holycross, cashier at the Coos-Curry Electric Cooperative office just across the street. From her office, she watches the pensioners show up for their midday card game and the community's working men arrive when the day's labor is done. Occasionally, she catches a glimpse of her husband, Ron, heading through the door.

"I think most women in town have a lot of curiosity about the place but they're not threatened," she says. "I've run over there to buy cigarettes a few times and it's a great place, like an old-fashioned barbershop must have been. Every day I see those older men show up. I know some of them don't even drink. Sometimes you see women come downtown to shop and drop their husbands off at Bill's. If your husband's going to have a beer, there couldn't be a better place."

Epilogue: Bill's Place, institution that it is, has not changed since 1986. Jimmy Agostino still deals pinochle. Harold Simmons still stops by for a beer. Burt Fry still watches out for the old men who live upstairs.

With jowls fit for royalty,
and a graying fringe that nibs over his collar,
he could be a movie version
of Senator Claghorn, or the favorite uncle
that drives a favorite aunt to distraction.

Harrisburg
Spring

THE SPEED MERCHANT

On an achingly beautiful April day, Elmer Skiles can be forgiven for laughing out loud. Not that he would ever apologize for his most persistent habit.

Who's to be sorry when the sun is laying its light on greening fields like new paint on a park bench and the aroma of cottonwood buds rises fresh from the riverside and, out ahead, a pair of tawny lightning bolts rocket through the grass just for the pure joy of running? So what if you're all of seventy-three. What if the bones do creak a bit and only last Christmas one of the greyhounds cut in front of you at thirty-five miles an hour and you dumped the motorized three-wheeler tailight-over-handlebars and bounced yourself into bed for a few days? Never mind. That was then and this is now, and spring is here and the sky is fresh-washed blue and see how those dogs run.

The wind plucks at his laughter and words as the machine jounces across the turf, the dogs teasing Skiles to crack the throttle so they can prove once again that canine muscle can out-accelerate Japanese horsepower. "Isn't that beautiful," he shouts. "Look at 'em go. They could be the ones, the ones that would be worth $20,000 some day. But how do you know? How do you really know? A lot of luck and a lot of hope, that's what it is. Other people play the lottery. But my odds are a lot better. And I have a lot more fun."

At least as much fun as Cheops and Rameses and King Tut had. The greyhound goes back that far, an arrow of a dog that could run fast as horses, a dog prized by rulers of those ancient civilizations. Surely no Pharaoh on camelback ever took more pleasure in running his greyhounds than does Elmer Skiles, skimming across a sun-shimmered grass field like some patriarchal cavalryman.

Around Harrisburg, only a few people understand the work Skiles does or the reputation it commands. In the small farming community that he calls home, Skiles is known as much for his humor as for the dogs that are prized by racing greyhound trainers around the nation. He reads widely, quotes the classic poets, writes some verse himself and loves deep philosophical discussions that, try as he might, he cannot help but end with some self-deprecating lancet of wit. With jowls fit for royalty, and a graying fringe that nibs over his collar, he could be a movie version of Senator Claghorn, or the favorite uncle that drives a favorite aunt to distraction. "If you talk to him for thirty minutes," says a former mayor of his town, "you'll be laughing for thirty-five."

Skiles would say that he is laughing last. He is a child of the Depression, a man whose life-track is like so many others from that era — seizing the main chance, moving from job to job, always showing a bit of restlessness. He grew up in Pennsylvania's Amish country, though historical circumstance saw to it that he never wore the plain clothes himself. He was saved for a different fate, perhaps, when a valued ancestor sought church membership and was judged "a horse racer, a fox chaser and a gambler."

Those genes are still strong. They were reined in, perhaps, for the thirty-year chunk of life in which Skiles moved through a variety of jobs, met and married his wife, Lillian, and raised six children. Along the way, he milked cows and fired railroad locomotives and built whiskey barrels and moved to Oregon. Still more jobs followed — farming, working as a state driver's license examiner, running his own driving school. "But the dogs have made me more than all those other jobs put together," he says. "And fun. A greyhound is just a long tail that will reach out and wrap around your heart."

Ah, yes, the dogs. In the early 1960s, a coworker introduced Skiles to greyhounds. The descendant of the horse racer and the fox chaser had never seen a greyhound running event and knew nothing about the world of competition and breeding. But it did not matter. The tail already was around his heart.

"I got out after the first batch of pups," he says. "But then I got right back in. I found out about raising greyhounds and dealing with the people who raise them. It's money and emotion, and that's a witches' brew. There were some tough years, and when I look back, I honestly don't know where the money came from or how we survived. But we did. I think I was more interested in the dogs than the money."

Though he would be nearly sixty before he met real success, Skiles plunged deeply into the world of greyhound racing. He went into business full-time and even took a fling at running a racing kennel for a season in Yuma. He learned, too, about the odd counterpressures of the greyhound breed. Winners are supremely competitive but docile, fast but not furious. No matter how speedy, the aggressive dog that causes problems on the track will show up in the disqualification column, not the winner's circle.

By 1972, Skiles was a breeder to be reckoned with. He was producing dogs that were winning big, some of them hauling in up to $25,000 a season on Florida and Arizona tracks. He settled into a role as one of the sport's prominent breeders, a man whose uncommon approach to the dogs produced uncommon results. In greyhound racing, breeders produce and raise dogs to maturity, then lease them to racing kennels under formulas that call for a sharing of prize money won in races. It is a world where the fainthearted do not play and the naive can lose their shirts.

It is also a world where, over the years, Skiles has established a reputation as a skillful breeder, a man with an uncanny rapport with dogs. Old track hands say that his greatest strength may be in the fifteen months of early training he gives dogs before they go to racing kennels. A few of the track veterans — like Martha

Hinkley, a prominent racing kennel operator on the Florida and West Virginia circuits—have been to Harrisburg to see Skiles and his charges romping in the ryegrass fields and working on a practice track.

"He has a tremendous reputation and he's produced some great dogs," Hinkley says. "Everybody knows that he has some very unorthodox ways of dealing with his dogs and that he spends an incredible amount of time with them just because he likes to do it. He's the only man I've ever seen who can turn a bunch of greyhounds loose and have them follow him instead of just taking off. It's certainly true that he has a very good line of dogs. But I've seen people buy into that line and then not be able to get nearly as much out of the dogs as he does. He just doesn't do things in the usual way."

Nor quite so actively in the eighth decade of his life. There was a time when the Skiles farm north of Harrisburg was home to fifty or so dogs, a time when Elmer and Lillian Skiles were on the road for months each year, delivering dogs to faraway trainers. But these days, the greyhound contingent numbers closer to fifteen, although the traveling schedule remains heavy. The years pass, and—on the long winter days—there is earnest talk over the kitchen table about how long this lovely foolishness with the dogs can go on.

"I'm fatalistic enough to believe that life follows a pattern," says the man who runs the greyhounds. "Maybe there were things I could have controlled, but I generally didn't. They just happened and created a situation that brought me a whole lot of happiness. How can I ever quit?"

Epilogue: Elmer Skiles gave up his beloved dogs, sold them off in 1987 as a concession to his age. It lasted only a while and then, with a grandson, he was back in operation. Two of his greyhounds were big winners on the Colorado circuit during the 1988 season.

It may be historical destiny playing
out in a tiny southern Oregon workshop,
where a man proves his mastery of skills
his long-ago countrymen made famous.

*Eagle Point
Summer*

THE ARTISAN

Clearly, the man likes machinery

For most of a working lifetime, he logged and sawmilled and ranched and bulldozed. And even today, at seventy-nine, there are few things that appeal more than jumping aboard one of his vintage motorcycles and roaring off on a long-distance jaunt. But the massive, work-worn hands of Victor Gardener do finer, more exacting work now. And there are places in the world where his name in its Italian version—Vittore Giardineri—is a synonym for art, for quality, and for a compulsion to put fine instruments in the hands of promising musicians.

Victor Gardener builds violins.

With simple tools from Sears-Roebuck, he made a few as a Jackson County farm boy more than half a century ago. And then he put the pursuit aside for a lifetime of wresting a living from Oregon's land. "But I always had the violins in my mind. All those years I was working in the woods and running equipment, I knew that I wanted to get back to making violins. I kept my tools. When I built my house, I made space for the shop. I knew I would do it again."

And now he does. In 1960, this son of an Italian stonemason sold off his ranch and his earthmoving equipment and retreated to work so fine that some of his tools resemble scalpels. Now, the violins and violas and cellos that flow from his hands are prized by professional musicians in Europe and North America.

"He's a world-class violin maker, an American legend even though he likes to use his Italian name," says Henry Siegle, former concertmaster of Washington's Bellevue and Seattle symphonies. "He did all those other things for so much of his life. He was a farmer and a bulldozer operator—every time I think about him and the bulldozer, the idea just kills me. He's lived this full life and done all these things and now, very late, he's mastered this craft. And he does it out of love of music. He cares who gets his instruments, not how much they sell for."

With a face that looks as if it might have been carved by hands as talented as his own and an Old World outlook hinged on craftsmanship and a strong work ethic,

Victor Gardener lives now on a mountainside piece of the land that his father once homesteaded. But his travels take him around the world. He visits often with the master violin makers of Europe. A quartet of his pieces—two violins, a viola, and a cello—hang in an honored place in the museum of Cavalese, Italy, the home of his Giardineri ancestors. The story of the instruments and their values reveals much.

"I built them and gave them to the museum because I wanted them to be there," he says. "I told the people I thought they might be worth about $12,000. They had them appraised, for insurance or something, and it came out at $56,000."

The man who builds such creations grew up near Eagle Point in a poor immigrant farming family. He learned a bit about the violin from country fiddlers and tried his hand at playing. At nineteen, Gardener built a violin with his mail-order tools. Sears service was more personalized in those days, and someone in the big corporation put him in touch with an old master violin maker in Seattle. The boy and the artisan corresponded. Ultimately, Gardener hauled his violin northward to show to his long-distance mentor.

"I've often wondered what that old man really thought," he says. "But he didn't laugh. He encouraged me." Four more violins followed. One commanded a price of ten dollars. The work went on, along with some playing. At twenty-one, Gardener began taking playing lessons from a violin teacher in Medford.

"I had this idea that I was going to play better than Jascha Heifetz, who was famous then," he says. "But I'd learned too many things the wrong way from the old fiddlers. It was too difficult to correct. To reach the level of music I wanted . . . it just wasn't there. I was starting to work then. There wasn't any way to keep a violin in a logging camp. So I gave up on competing with Heifetz. But I never stopped thinking about making violins. I always thought about that."

However, for thirty-five years his tools were in storage. He married his wife, Harriet, raised a family, and pursued logging, lumbering, surveying, and ranching. The ranch that he established after World War II did so well that he was able to begin easing into a comfortable retirement in his mid-fifties. In his small shop, he turned out twenty violins before he had one that satisfied him. In the twenty-five years since then, he has produced three hundred instruments, a total that only a handful of instrument builders in America have reached.

"A few instrument makers helped me when I started again," he says. "But that's not customary. There are a lot of jealous people with crazy secrets in this business. I think a lot of those secrets aren't worth anything. They talk about working only with hundred-year-old wood, and they brag about their secret varnishes that probably aren't worth carrying home. And they want to get $5,000 for each violin. A man can make a living without charging more than $1,500."

Above all else, the image of Gardener-as-American-legend has been fueled by his approach to pricing. His work ranks with those instruments that sell for $5,000 to $10,000. But his price structure is simple: $500 for a violin, $700 for a viola, $1,500 for a cello. A cello represents three hundred hours of work.

"I know I'm way underpriced," he says. "But I remember when I wanted a fiddle and couldn't afford one. There are a lot of young, talented people out there like that. I do this because I like it and because I want to help people. Other makers ding me for doing it. But I do it anyhow. The amount of instruments I make at my price is not going to hurt the world market."

"I know I'm way underpriced. But I remember when I wanted a fiddle and couldn't afford one. There are a lot of young, talented people out there. I do this because I want to help people."

In Seattle, Siegle chuckles in wonderment when he talks of the selling of the Giardineri instruments. "Some people say that he's well off and doesn't need the money, and maybe he's writing it off on his taxes," Siegle says. "I know he's shrewd. But he's the only maker I know who cares so much about who gets his instruments and what they will do with them. I've met very few people who listen to music the way he does. He truly loves music. This is his contribution."

Though Gardener is critical of some modern instrument makers, he has only reverence for the old Italian master artisans, such as Antonio Stradivari and Giuseppi Guarneri. His work, patterned on theirs, seldom deviates from the lessons of the centuries. His reverence, however, does not extend to European wood. The maple and spruce of the Northwest, from high elevation stands that he scouts and logs personally, are the heart of his work. He has stockpiled enough select cuts for another lifetime of work. It remains his fashion to make light of those who would attach too much mystique to a process that, for him, is fundamentally a matter of craftsmanship.

"For a while I bought wood from Europe," he says. "It was too expensive. It is not any better. Now it's gone. The Europeans are getting wood from America. They're selling it to instrument makers here and telling them it's European."

As he nears eighty, Gardener's only concern is his eyes. His hands are steady. His health and agility are those of a younger man. With the instruments, as with the motorcycles, he has no intention of slowing down. "I don't play the violin anymore," he says. "I put music in other people's hands. That's what I do. I try to spread joy and music."

Epilogue: Victor Gardener has a year-and-a-half's worth of instrument orders awaiting him.

Loggers and farmers, most of them,
and long past their athletic prime,
but every summer they crank it up
and bruise each other with abandon,
just for the memories.

Coquille
Summer

ONE MORE TIME

Late in the game, a churning Coquille ballcarrier with fire in his eye and the goal line in reach tried to turn the corner. Defensive end Doug Curtis, Sr., wearing the blue of the Myrtle Point Bobcats, nailed him. And Doug Curtis, Jr., was the second defender on the tackle. Father and son, age forty-four and age twenty-two. The man from the woods and the student home from college. They eyed each other for a second, grinned, and trotted back to the defensive huddle together. Later, as post-game flashbulbs popped and on-field rivals renewed off-field friendships, the father was still savoring the play.

"I couldn't have asked God Himself for a better moment," he said, with his helmet tucked under a grass-stained elbow and a cigarette dangling from his fingertips. "To be in the fourth quarter of a good game and be in on the same tackle with your son and have him look at you in a way that you know he's proud of you. It was great. I'm not as fast anymore as some of these guys and not as strong, but I've had more fun than anybody."

Welcome to the Coquille-Myrtle Point alumni football game, an epic and thoroughly physical contest wherein loggers and farmers and millworkers from a pair of blue-collar small towns shuck their overalls and work boots in favor of the high school uniforms and pads and helmets they put aside so long ago. It is *Sometimes a Great Notion* in pads, the juncture where the glow of memory meets the reality of passing years.

"It's insanity," says Lynn Schrag, forty-three, of Coquille. "I know I can't keep up with these young bucks. But it's just such a kick to suit up one more time for old CHS, even if your wife is sitting up in the stands shaking her head."

This one is for keeps, for bragging rights until next August, for the renewal of a bitter high school rivalry that stretches back toward the beginnings of the present century. It is a nostalgic contest that raises a respectable amount of money for the two schools' athletic departments and brings yesteryear's heroes back to the scenes — if not the physical condition — of their former glory. Does it all mean anything? "Two years ago, we lost this game 2-0 and I cried," said Jim Barrett, a twenty-six-year-old defensive end who suits up most days for a plywood layup team at a mill in Coquille.

Old-grad football games, where one school or one town takes on another, were common in Oregon decades ago. But liability concerns, along with the television age that made the games less of a draw than they once were, have nearly eliminated them from the state's sports scene. The Coquille-Myrtle Point contest is perhaps the best of the alumni contests that remain.

It is a natural, for many reasons. Start with a pair of gritty little Coast Range towns, with slow-paced timber and agriculture-based economies that keep many grads of the two small high schools close to home, the kind of places where an ex-halfback in his fifties may see his quarterback every morning at the post office or the coffee shop. Stir in the facts that the two communities, nearly equal in size, are only ten miles apart on Highway 42 and that their high school football records against each other are almost dead-even after decades of bruising play. The rivalry between the schools runs deep indeed in families that have sent generations of players onto the field.

In the early 1980s, Coquille grads Bill Head and Spike Parry, perhaps with painful memories blunted by the passage of time, decided that football should not end at graduation. They pulled together an alumni team, worked out nettlesome insurance details with the Coquille School District, borrowed the school's gear and scheduled a game with Bandon. Timber fallers came down from the hills and farmers came in from the fields for the Coquille practices. That first squad ranged from a logger of fifty-two to an eighteen-year-old scatback only a year past graduation. "It was a great experience for everybody," said Head, a thirty-eight-year-old logger. "That first year we went full contact in the first practice with no pads. There was blood everywhere. It was great."

Bandon bowed out after two lopsided wins by Coquille's alumni Red Devils. So Head and Parry, doing what they had wanted to do in the first place, issued the challenge to arch-rival Myrtle Point. Maybe it was not the best idea. The old Bobcats from the town down the road put together a strong, fast team that shut out Coquille 2-0 and 32-0 in successive years. For 1988, practices opened on the towns' high school fields more than two weeks before the game. Some players had started their conditioning months earlier. At a practice a few nights before the game, the Bobcats' head coach, Craig Johnson, a Myrtle Point teacher, talked about what the annual battle had become.

"You can't believe how pumped up these guys get," he said. "It's a chance for them to relive the past and see if they can beat Coquille one more time. When the hitting starts, it's amazing. The first year we had broken noses, snapped tendons, broken ribs, shoulder separations, stitches, everything. I'm Coquille, class of '66. They call me Benedict Johnson over there. But I'm not playing. If I played, I'd have to play for Coquille and go against these animals I'm coaching."

For Johnson and for Coquille coach Ken Trathen, the $1,000 a year that the game generates for each school's athletic fund is reason enough to play the game. The money is used for a variety of purposes, from purchasing a pair of football shoes for a kid from a poor family, to buying special training equipment that the school budget cannot finance.

Two decades past his high school football career, Wayne VanBurger, a Coquille Red Devil once more, savors a new victory and a post-game moment with his son, Ty. The annual August benefit game between the alumni of the neighboring towns of Myrtle Point and Coquille is a community event that fills the stands and gives old grads a chance to replay the exploits of their youth.

With home-field advantage, the twice-beaten Coquille alums welcomed their rivals from down the road on a late-summer Saturday night that provided cool, fallish, footballish weather. A thousand fans found seats in the stands and scanned their programs for old schoolboy heroes. The trappings that have made the game a community happening were much in evidence. Coquille's Chevrolet dealership had gleaming new pickups displayed on the track, prizes from local merchants were ready for raffling, hairdresser Judy Gardner was priming for her *a capella* rendition of the national anthem.

On a stairway outside the Coquille locker room, Rick Yeager, twenty-eight, sat alone in his crimson Coquille uniform, hands clenched, staring into the middle distance, his mind a dozen years off in the past. "Trying to get psyched up, like I did in high school," he said. "I started getting ready for this a month ago. I've lost twelve pounds. I've been running. There's a lot of pride in this game. Some of us want vengeance for the last couple years."

Wayne Vanberger, thirty-seven, a Coquille graduate who is the wrestling coach at Marshfield High School in neighboring Coos Bay, shrugged into his uniform with thoughts that blended gratitude and philosophy. "This game is a payback," Vanberger said. "This is the town that made it possible for me to have my own high school athletic career. Now I can repay it. This is the kind of thing I always preach to my athletes."

In the pre-game locker room talks, older warriors reminded younger ones of ancient victories and ancient defeats, of memories to be served, pride to be upheld, and embarrassment to be avoided. Recent memory made the coaches add cautions about fighting. And Trathen could not resist tempering the intensity of his Coquille warriors just a bit. "Remember," he said, "they may look big, but they're just as out of shape as we are."

The game was a wonder. Lunch-bucket carriers became ball carriers. Men who felled trees in their workaday lives felled runners with the same precision. Log truckers, bulldozer operators, even a few white-collar guys, thumped each other mightily at the line. Offensive execution was good and major defensive breakdowns were minimal. Players who had graduated since the late 1970s played the early minutes, but the quality of play did not fall off much when the 35-and-older players were stirred into the mix. In the main, it was youth in the backfield and age on the line.

Coquille served notice that it would be no patsy when it punched across a touchdown and a two-point conversion midway through the first period. Myrtle Point put six of its own on the board with a slick pass play in the second. In the early going, Bobcat tackle Jim Mast—who's thirty-four, 6 feet 2 inches, and 350 pounds—launched himself skyward to bat down a Coquille pass. "Hey, fat boys fly," he laughed as he came back to the bench.

"When he looked down and saw he was off the ground, he was scared to death," said his brother, John.

On Coquille's sideline, alumni yell leaders romped in the outfits they once wore. Some of them mixed the demands of cheering with the necessities of caring for their children. Zana Boyer, a graduate in Coquille's class of 1983, was balancing her daughter, Lacey, on one hip and getting her first good look at her husband Brian, class of 1978, in uniform. "We graduated five years apart. This is the first chance I've ever had to yell for him in a game," she said. "For years, I've wished I could have done that."

In the second half, Myrtle Point scored early on another pass play but again flubbed the conversion to run the count to 12-8. The intensity level rose. The referees broke up several scuffles, assessed a couple of unsportsmanlike conduct penalties, and ejected a Coquille player.

At the Myrtle Point bench between series, lineman Vern Breuer, forty-one, of Chandler, Arizona, was gleeful, and not just about the score. "It's incredible what a release this is," Breuer said. "I played one year in college and I figured I'd never put on a uniform again. Last year they called me from up here and that was all it took. I got a plane and headed up. I'm back this year and I'll be here next year. I wouldn't miss it."

Perhaps in some other year his Myrtle Point team would do better. It failed to score after the mid-point of the third quarter. The Bobcats watched in futility as Coquille punched in three more touchdowns. The tally stood at 27-12 at the final horn. For the next half-hour, players who had been ready to duke it out slapped backs, shook hands, and congratulated each other for surviving another game. Watching it all, the Coquille grad who steered the Myrtle Point team felt neither traitorous nor disappointed.

"Really, if you consider what this game is all about, this is good," Johnson said. "The game was competitive. But if we had won, it would be 3-0, our favor. That might make it hard for these Coquille guys to get a team together next year. This way it's 2-1. Both towns have something to prove. That means this will go on. Next year, everybody's gonna want back on the field."

Epilogue: In a physical examination a day after the game, Bill Head learned that damage to his knee had ended his post-high school football career. From the sidelines, he continues as organizer and promoter of the annual Coquille-Myrtle Point alumni game.

The place by the bay
is a treasure chest, tastefully filled
to overflowing with the memories
and the booty from the travels
of two well-lived lifetimes.

North Bend
Winter

Realized Dreams

THE SHIP WILL NEVER WEIGH ANCHOR, never leave port. Rooted to earth as firmly as the giant myrtle that grows just off its starboard rail, it trembles a bit when the wakes of ocean-bound freighters tickle the foot of the hillside that holds it forever fifty feet above the waters of Coos Bay.

Ah, but the voyages its crew has made.

And the treasures they have brought from faraway lands: here an Easter Island totem, there a prize green conch shell from the West Indies, and there a glimmering ceremonial robe from old China. Ship models and paintings and statuary and African carvings and pre-Columbian artifacts and feather money from the South Seas. All of it, room after room of it, ten thousand square feet of it, rides easily aboard the Pleasant Point. Captain John stares wooden-eyed and serene across the bay, assured of smooth sailing aboard a vessel where the compass heading on the brass binnacle will never change.

The ship's cargo is the record not of one variegated, eclectic, much-traveled lifetime, but of two. Like all sea stories, this one is full of surprises, as unpredictable as a bar crossing in a gale. Where to start in telling of the voyages of Edna Skinner, the Broadway, Hollywood, and television actress, and Jean Fish, the high-fashion model and designer? How is it that two sixty-five-year-old women whose pasts are laden with glamor and glitter and world travels – not to mention ranching and diving and big-time sport fishing and a few other gritty adventures – have come to set anchor in Coos County?

The answers reside in the house above the bay. The house that is a boat, or the boat that is a house.

"This is the way we planned it," says Edna Skinner, known to those of one generation as a star in television's *Mr. Ed* and to those of another as a star in the original Broadway company of the musical, *Oklahoma!* The house was to be an expression of our lives and the way we've lived. We wanted it to show the things we've always done."

One of the things that they had always done, these two whimsical women who have been friends for more than thirty years, is travel — with their husbands when they were married and together after they were each widowed. And much of that travel, especially in the 1940s and 1950s, was done by sea. "Both of us had been all over the world by ship," says Jean Fish, once known as Susan King, the model and fashion designer whose face, work, and newspaper columns received national recognition forty years ago. "It was an important part of our lives. We both have very precious memories about good things that happened aboard ships. And now we have our own ship."

But still, this moorage is an unlikely home port for Jean Fish, who only a few short years ago owned the Palm Springs, California, house that had been the retreat of Greta Garbo and John Gilbert; or for Edna Skinner, who once was certain that she would never leave the Montana ranch that she suppported with her stage and screen earnings.

Edna was born in Washington, D.C. In the pre-World War II era, she was educated at the American Academy of Dramatic Arts in New York, with class-mates such as Kirk Douglas, Lauren Bacall, and Jennifer Jones. She did summer stock as a young woman and later played vaudeville and club shows. When *Oklahoma!* hit the U.S. stage, she landed a job in the Chicago company of the play and later replaced Celeste Holm for the final year of the musical's run in New York. During World War II, she was heavily involved in USO tours and other volunteer entertainment efforts for American troops.

After the war, Skinner appeared regularly in movies and television. She worked before the cameras for films like *Friendly Persuasion* and *Easy to Love.* Her television credits included *Topper, The Great Gildersleeve, Daniel Boone,* and *The Millionaire.* But she is perhaps best known as Kay Addison, the acerbic neighbor in *Mr. Ed,* the early 1960s television comedy built on the antics of a talking horse.

During her Hollywood years, Edna and her husband, Bob Turner, who was an importer, owned a Montana ranch. "Basically, we kept going back to Hollywood to support the ranch," she says. "It was kind of crazy. We were working for the cows and horses." In those years, Skinner discovered the joys of fishing. She plunged substantial portions of her earnings and her travel time into it. Her name soon began to appear in American fishing record books. Recognized as an expert, she began writing for outdoor publications.

Jean Fish, meanwhile, had grown up in a Southern California hotel and restaurant family. She was taking voice lessons and seriously considering a singing career when a modeling agency offered her a contract. Fish spent ten years in the world of high fashion. For most of that time, she worked exculsively for the Maurice Everett label. As Susan King — designer, model, and newspaper fashion columnist — she became the Everett line's most recognizable symbol. Some of her work from that time evoked memories of the fashion of the 1920s. That style is still her personal signature.

Fish's first marriage ended in divorce. Her second was to the Rev. Joseph Arthur Fish, pastor of the large and prestigious Pico-Arlington Christian Church in Los Angeles. As she eased out of the world of fashion, Jean found new careers in television animation and interior design. Her circle of Hollywood acquaintances

From atop the bow of the Pleasant Point, Jean Fish and Edna Skinner enjoy a perfect vantage for watching ships that call at Coos Bay and for recalling their own travels to far-flung ports. Although their home displays hundreds of mementos and trophies from those excursions, it offers few reminders of their earlier careers, such as Edna's long-running role in a television series.

was wide – Liberace played at her wedding, and Ethel Merman was a close friend. So was Edna Skinner. And, in the mid-1970s, after Robert Turner and Joseph Fish had died, the two women began traveling together regularly.

Long before then, Skinner had risen to national prominence in the sport fishing world. Teaming with her sister, Ann, a photographer, she worked for a variety of outdoor publications and tackle companies. After Ann Skinner died, Jean Fish taught herself photography and, though it was something she would never have envisioned, learned fishing from Edna. Soon her name also was appearing in the sports record books. The pair braved white water and cold water and ocean surf.

In the tropics, Edna added diving to her repertoire, and amassed a huge collection of rare shells which she catalogued with museum precision. Once, she nearly died from a case of the bends in a diving mishap. For a decade, the two women ranged the world – fishing, writing, and buying art objects and antiques. Then, in 1975, they decided they were ready for a change.

Fishing expeditions to Oregon had made Edna fond of the state, so the pair agreed to buy a cabin at Lakeside, the tiny community between Coos Bay and Reedsport, on the Oregon Coast. Soon they were in the antique business. The Dockside, the Lakeside store they created and filled with European and American antiques, was a popular tourist spot for most of a decade. But after two years the cabin was too small, the business was too large, and the concept of splitting each year between Oregon and California was too difficult. It was decision time. Jean laughs when she recalls it.

"I almost won," she says. "We had this beautiful home in Palm Springs, with a live-in housekeeper and everything we needed. It seemed so sophisticated and perfect to try to keep it and use it for part of each year. But we decided to start house hunting."

With their tastes, possessions, and resources, not just any house would do. They ranged Coos County for months, almost despairing of finding a place that would fit their vision. And then they discovered a two-year-old, four thousand-square-foot home perched on a point above the waters of Coos Bay. It was a start. With Jean as designer, they plunged into an eleven-month whirlwind of construction that would more than double the size of the place and create the nautical fantasy they had decided upon.

"There was never really a set of blueprints at the start," Jean says. "We hired people, and I worked with them. As a designer, I could envision the way something would look when it was finished. Each part just evolved out of talking with the workers." The biggest change was the construction of a 131-foot ship hull against one side of the original house. The two-deck vessel has a foredeck viewing area, a salon, a bar and a large kitchen on its main deck. Topside is the bridge, with the life-sized wooden ship's captain standing at the helm, surveying a panoply of gleaming brass instruments.

"There was no ego involved in doing this," Edna Skinner says, as she recalls the creation of their home. "We weren't looking to have the biggest house on the bay. We just wanted a place that would be beautiful and that would be a place for the things that are important to us. There are a lot of faces in this house. A lot of people work to keep it going."

The finished product is a tribute to the expansive tastes of the two women, to the lives they have led and to Fish's design talent in pulling it all together. What could have come off as a fusty collection of bric-a-brac or a sterile museum has instead the aura of a home, a dwelling where fantasies and realized dreams and everyday living merge comfortably. Improbable as it sounds, a decor that ranges from world-record bass to New Guinea tribal masks to a saddlebag from Custer's last battlefield has been made to work.

Show business memorabilia is conspicuous by its near-absence. A few *Mr. Ed* mementos in Skinner's office and some old modeling photographs buried in a room crammed with Fish's exquisite doll collection are the only testimony to the careers that made the house possible.

The home has never been open for tours. Unannounced visitors are politely turned away. But in the Coos Bay area, the place has become something of a public resource. It has been used frequently to entertain visiting dignitaries in the area's economic development efforts. For Skinner and Fish, the travels never seem to stop. The home's eclectic collection continues to grow, swelling with the trophies of each new trip. And the task of managing the whole unlikely enterprise — with help that ranges from housekeepers to security personnel who patrol the grounds at night — remains a welcome one.

"For two women to keep this place going is about like running a hotel," Edna Skinner says. "We love it. But it takes strength and stamina and commitment."

Epilogue: The traveling continues, now with an emphasis on preserving the earth and its creatures. Since 1986, Edna and Jean have regularly journeyed from the Arctic to the tropics on behalf of polar bears, harp seals, and dolphins. A diving foray in the Caribbean, a voyage by ship to China and an extended visit to Costa Rica have all produced new treasures for the house.

Rounding up cattle or the tales
of the past, a cowboy at
Oregon's far eastern edge works every day
to preserve a treasured way of life.

Jordan Valley
Autumn

THE HISTORIAN

He was hanging out in the bar at the old Jordan Valley Hotel when other kids were playing Little League baseball. Wide-eyed, he listened there to the tales of aging cowhands and ancient Basque sheepherders, rheumy-eyed men who had known the wagon train families, the Indian fighters, the cattle barons. For Mike Hanley, cowboy and rancher, the listening has not stopped for thirty-five years. One day he is up in the saddle, working cows in the sagebrush; the next, he is off rounding up history, taking notes from some cattle country oldtimer who has tales to tell.

"This is a way of life that's disappearing," he says. "We're losing pieces of it all the time. I'm just trying to save as much of it as I can." Hanley is a college-educated cowboy whose family roots go deep into the eastern Oregon rangeland. At forty-six, he is historian and researcher, artist and author, blacksmith and stonemason. But most of all, he is a man with a mission.

In every Western town, there are those who will idly say that somebody should get to the oldtimers and collect their stories before they die. It seldom happens. But Hanley does it. He has been at it for so long now that he has moved from one generation of oldtimers to the next. Call it telling the stories of the Old West—and the New West—from the ranchers' point of view. Catching history before it goes a-glimmering. Bringing its lessons home to the twentieth century, where Hanley and a new generation of ranchers often confront a public that won't make the leap from the romance of the past to the realities of the present.

He is two books into his mission already, with another headed to the publisher and still another in the works. All of them done with a straightforward, anecdotal sort of style, a kind of campfire storytelling in print. For Hanley, it is a mission, not a hobby.

He was barely nine when it began, on a cattle drive out of Jordan Valley with his father. He slept beside the fire with grizzled old range riders whose memories stretched back to late nineteenth-century Indian battles, mining boom towns and the exploits of cattle kings like Pete French and John Devine. "On that drive, I wrote down the first story," Hanley says. "I used the stub of a pencil from my dad's tally book and I wrote it on the back of a label off a tomato can."

From there, he was off and running. No oldtimer was safe. From the bar at the hotel to ranches in the hills, he searched them out, heard their stories and took diligent notes. He did it all the way through grade school and high school, and sometimes the results showed up in papers he wrote for his teachers. Slowly, he built his collection of information on the early settlement days of the I-O-N country, the desert region where portions of Idaho, Oregon, and Nevada share history and geography.

"I started thinking about a book when I was still in high school," he says. "Before long I knew it was going to take at least four books. And that's still the plan." He knew nothing, of course, about the business of writing and publishing books when he headed off to Eastern Oregon State College at the age of eighteen. Professor Lee Johnson and other faculty members at the school were amazed at the formidable body of information the new student had assembled. They channeled his efforts and pointed out new directions. "He was a diamond in the rough," says Johnson, who is now retired. "He came out of one of those fine pioneer families from that Malheur country. He showed up with all of this knowledge about that area and no real understanding of how to get it all written. So some of us worked with him on it."

Hanley's first book, *Owhyee Trails,* began taking form while he was still in college, although the volume was not published until 1973. Northwest writer Ellis Lucia aided Hanley in the final stages of pulling the material together and is listed as coauthor. Hanley's second work, *Sagebrush and Axle Grease,* was a solo project. So is his third, which will be titled *Tales of the I-O-N Country.* The books recount the history of a section of the West so isolated that pioneer settlement began decades later than in other parts of Oregon. Indian wars raged until 1878. Mining boom towns flourished into the 1890s. New homesteaders were still coming into the area after 1900. Hanley's history is told through people. Bannock and Paiute Indians. Scotch and Irish ranchers. Basque sheepherders and Chinese miners. Prospectors and prostitutes.

In his more recent writings, he has worked to tie the past to the present. He and other ranchers of the I-O-N country, no matter how large their holdings, depend on federal grazing land. These days, ranchers compete with those who have other purposes and other ideas, from recreationists to environmentalists to vandals.

"I think I spend about a quarter of my time either working or thinking on things that have to do with the government and the land," he says. "For years we've let other people who are more vocal do the writing and the talking about this land. We've taken what we know about the land and this way of life for granted. I guess I'm trying to change that. I want to show how we got to be here and why we belong here. Our ancestors made this land work and made it what it is. In America, the majority rules. I think that eventually, if the majority of the people feels there's no longer any need for us out here, they'll remove us. I'm trying to show that we have some historical vested rights to be here."

If that was all that Hanley was doing it would be work enough, because it comes on top of the consuming task of running a 2,400-acre ranch. But his projects

Mike Hanley's mix of history and work plays out in many ways, including buckboard rides with his wife, Linda. Though it takes a bit longer than using a pickup truck, the Hanleys find it a pleasant way to check fences and feed stock on their ranch. Unlike many ranchers, Hanley looks for ways to maintain horses and antique equipment as integral parts of his cattle operation.

gallop off in all directions, like cattle in a lightning storm. Stashed around the ranch are thirty wagons, buckboards, Conestogas, and stagecoaches that Hanley has rebuilt from the ground up. To do it, he has made himself a blacksmith, a wheelwright, and a carpenter. Most of the wagons come to him as a jumble of rusted parts and rotted wood. All of them have historic significance, connections with pioneer families or historic figures from the region.

"People just bring them," he says. "Sometimes I'll come home and there'll be the remains of an old wagon dumped in front of the shop. Or someone will die, and the family won't know what to do with the old wagon that's parked out behind the barn, so they give it to me." Hanley's wagon works is a masonry building of the buff-colored sandstone that once was commonly used in eastern Oregon structures. He crafted the place, stone by stone, from the rubble of a dance hall that was demolished in Jordan Valley.

A few years ago Hanley helped locate and mark the lost grave of Jean Baptiste Charbonneau. The son of the Indian woman, Sacajawea, Charbonneau was born in 1805 on the Lewis and Clark expedition to the Pacific Coast. Charbonneau grew to adulthood and remained in the West. He was traveling from California to Montana in 1866 when he died near Jordan Valley and was buried at a place known locally as the Ruby Ranch.

When Hanley completed that project, he knew it was time to turn to others. On and on it goes. Hanley is attempting to get sections of the historic Bell A Ranch near Burns onto the National Register of Historic Places. He is seeking a way to preserve a crumbling Basque pelota, or handball, court in Jordan Valley. He takes speaking engagements and tours school children around his ranch. Much of his work in recent years has been directed at preserving the history of the Basque, the strong and colorful shepherds who immigrated in the 1880s from the Pyrenees of Spain to the I-O-N country. Thoroughly Americanized and intermarried with the region's ranching and business families, the present generation of Basques have only a tenuous hold on the culture of their ancestors.

"I'm not a Basque, but I work real hard to preserve their heritage," Hanley says. "It's not just their heritage now. It's our heritage, too, just like all of these things I'm trying to capture. That's why I do this work."

Epilogue: Since 1987, Mike Hanley has published his third book. He continues to be heavily involved in the running battle over use of public lands for livestock grazing.

"We've let other people who are more vocal do the writing and the talking about this land," Mike Hanley says. "We've taken what we know about the land and this way of life for granted."

The sailor and the railroader have long been
heralded in song, but a duo
of Oregon loggers makes musical room
for another kind of working man.

Deadwood
Summer

SAWDUST AND MUSIC

SCREAMING SAWS, CRASHING TREES and roaring trucks they can handle. But that pales beside what they can accomplish with acoustic guitars and mellow voices. Still, the idea of taking their music to market was always more fearful than any of the dangers of the woods. For years, Craig Jenkins and Terry McKinnis were self-taught, aw-shucks musicians—the kind of pickers who would duck their heads, grin sheepish grins and strum another tune every time someone suggested they should do something with the original material that was flowing out of their heads and off their fingertips.

But finally they put aside their tools and their reservations. Almost to their own surprise, the result was an album that proved to be a polished mix of deft picking, smooth singing and graceful lyrics that captured the logger's life. And— no surprise to those who had been listening to the two guitar-playing, songwriting buddies for years—the thing sold. For a couple of quiet woodsmen, it was a problem. The furor was enough to make a man want to pick up his saw and retreat to the safety of the woods.

"We've never thought of ourselves as professional musicians," Craig said. "We don't read music. We have to memorize everything we write. We just work on something until it sounds good. We do it for our own enjoyment and for the people around us. Now we've got people buying these things ten and twenty at a time. And there's a big logging supply company down in California that's talking about doing a distribution deal. We never planned for this."

Their tape album, "The Snag Fallers Ball," is a mostly light-hearted collection of songs about logging in Oregon and Alaska. Jenkins wrote nine of the eleven songs on the album and coauthored two others with Don Beck, a friend who also is a logger and musician. Jenkins and McKinnis do the singing on the album, with Craig's animated, Burl Ives-like voice dominant.

The material on the album deals with such woods scenarios as the foibles of family-owned logging operations, the logger's propensity to quit any job that does

---

not suit him, and the frustrations of a weary choker setter. The songs are laced with the jargon of the woods. Loggers give the album high marks for authenticity.

Terry McKinnis met Craig's sister, Kim, and married her in 1977. The two men have been playing guitar together ever since. McKinnis had been a casual player since his junior high years. Jenkins had started even earlier, singing and playing around the family piano with some uncles who were logger-musicians. Although both Craig and Terry did some dabbling with rock, they gravitated early to folk and gospel music. After they met, they discovered they had been walking the same musical trail.

"We played in a lot of churches, grange meetings, funerals, weddings, talent programs, all kinds of things," McKinnis says. "People like Gordon Lightfoot had influenced us a lot. We both like him but we didn't realize how much it showed until other people started noticing that sound in our music."

Craig Jenkins, a native of Deadwood in the Coast Range west of Eugene, went to the woods after graduating from high school. He worked in Alaska and in Oregon before becoming a partner in an independent logging outfit. At thirty-five, he works daily in the timber, rides a sparkling Harley-Davidson and spends a surprising amount of time listening to classical music. McKinnis, who is thirty-four, graduated from high school in the coastal town of Waldport, logged for a decade, then hired on with a construction company that builds logging roads. He is a motorcyclist, too, and he and Jenkins have been known to head off for a wedding gig with guitars strapped to their big bikes.

In the picking and singing sessions that became routine for them after they met, they began to dabble in creating lyrics and melodies of their own. Craig Jenkins characterizes much of that work as a diversion and describes most of the songs as pieces that were done for one-time special occasions. But the music found ready audiences in western Lane County. "I was writing a few tunes and we were playing at some places and packing them in," Craig says. "We started getting a few offers from outfits like the Rodeway Inns. I figured it was time to make a decision. So I did. I went with a logging company up in Alaska."

But friends always made it difficult for them to edge away from the idea of recording some of their work. And the idea of crafting a collection of songs about logging was intriguing. For decades, the coal miners and the cowboys, the sailors and the railroaders have been well served by folk musicians. But the men who work the woods mostly have gone unheralded in song. The work of the late Buzz Martin, recorded more than twenty years ago, generally is regarded as the only significant collection of logging music.

"I met him once," Craig says. "He was from Five Rivers, about two ridges over from here. He'd done lots of logging songs, he'd toured with Johnny Cash, things like that. We got together and picked up guitars one day. Ate popcorn and played some songs. It was a good time. It kind of inspired me. I mean, he was a logger— basically a blue-collar type of person—and he'd done something."

Later, Jenkins and Beck teamed to write "Snag Fallers' Ball," the song that would become the album's title track. That tune and others went over well around the small towns of Florence and Mapleton, and increased the already-frequent suggestions that McKinnis and Jenkins do something serious with their work. Finally, out of excuses, they committed themselves to doing it. For Jenkins, it was a decision that suddenly took songwriting out of the casual mode and made it serious work. He and McKinnis decided they needed eight new songs for the album. For the first time, they found themselves creating against a deadline.

The recording business was a strange new world for them, as foreign as a Coast Range logging operation might be for a studio musician. After a false start or two, they found Doug Daniels in Eugene. Daniels, a blind folk musician who had established a small recording studio, made his own contributions. He convinced the apprehensive loggers to do what they do best, letting their voices and the acoustic guitars carry the songs in the best folk music tradition, rather than following the advice they had been getting about adding synthesizer sounds. And he also persuaded them to do the recordings live, like folk and jazz musicians traditionally have done, rather than laying down and blending separate tracks through studio wizardry.

"It was like two cultures meeting when we found him," Jenkins said. "We were just a couple of loggers with some music and we didn't know if he was going to laugh at us or what. But he took us seriously."

The partners invited Daniels to add his own guitar sounds to the mix. They also accepted some production delays that cost them the chance to unveil the album at Oregon's biggest logging convention. "I'm glad we didn't make it," McKinnis said. "The quality wouldn't have been there if we had pushed it through. Instead we took our time and satisfied ourselves with what we did."

Jenkins and McKinnis ordered up a thousand tapes, thinking that they might sell out in a matter of months or years. Though the album was placed only in a few chain saw shops and rural markets, the world — at least the logging world of the Northwest — beat a path to their post office box. Nonetheless, McKinnis and Jenkins have neither the delusion nor the desire that music will take them out of the woods. But they talk about another album. And about the possibility that they might do something to help preserve a way of life that they love.

"A lot of things go through my mind when I play the guitar in the evenings," Jenkins says. "The album doesn't really have anything controversial on it. But in the next one I'd like to address some issues about what's happening to the logger. I wouldn't do a whole album like that. Just a couple of songs. I think I could do it with a sense of humor that would take the edge off and communicate with people. If we do another album, I want to write about some things the logger's up against and what his future is."

They will call it "Endangered Species."

Epilogue: Since the summer of 1988, Craig Jenkins and Terry McKinnis have sold several thousand copies of their album. In February 1989, they combined with Doug Daniels and guitarist Neil Isaacson to produce the second album, "Endangered Species." Reviews have been favorable and sales have been brisk.

This matter of being Santa Claus
is nearly a year-round job and
a foolish pursuit, some would say,
but it is a role that has given
much to the giver.

*Junction City
Winter*

THE REAL SANTA CLAUS

I̲N̲ ̲H̲I̲S̲ ̲O̲W̲N̲ ̲C̲H̲I̲L̲D̲H̲O̲O̲D̲, this Santa did without Christmas.

So Red Johnson has spent a lifetime catching up. He has been Santa on ships at sea, in hospital wards where bright-eyed children spend their final Christmas, in nursing homes where ninety-year-olds deep into their second childhood climb onto his lap, at office parties where he sings and matches one-liners with the best and the brightest. Some who have seen him cavorting around Yuletide events in Junction City and nearby Eugene swear that he is the real Kriss Kringle.

The flowing hair and the whiskers are genuine, an eight-month crop grown annually for the duties of the Christmas season. But no less real is the attitude, which doesn't come off when the holidays end. Johnson gives away toys in July and, year-round, entertains children who drag playmates to his door to prove that Santa Claus lives behind it. "I know that a lot of people look at me and say, 'That old fool thinks he's really Santa Claus.' But I don't. All I'm really doing is keeping the spirit alive for other people."

No one did that for Red Johnson. The giver of good Christmas memories carries painful ones. The earliest holiday season he can remember was seventy years ago, when he was not quite four years old. A few days before that Christmas, he sat atop the kitchen table playing with a red and green paper chain — and saw his mother accidentally shot to death during a family squabble. The authorities then broke up the family. Johnson spent six years in a county orphanage. Then he was farmed out to help a Gallipolis, Ohio, family with the chores. "It wasn't a real home. It was next door to the school. When there was a recess, I had to go home and hoe the garden."

By the time he was sixteen, he was on his own, holding down a man's job on the barges of the Great Lakes. In the Depression, like so many young, single men of his time, he bounced across America. Christmases in those years found him riding the rails, working as a hired hand on western ranches and, finally, cooking in a Civilian Conservation Corps camp in the desert reaches of eastern Oregon. He traveled from there to Junction City, where he found a woods job and met his wife, Irene Smyth.

World War II provided them both with shipyard work in Portland. Before the war's end, Johnson shipped out as a merchant seaman, cooking aboard a Liberty ship. He would follow the sea, off and on, for twenty years. "I played Santa lots of times on the ships out in the Pacific. I did Neptune a few times, too, when we crossed the equator."

On land, he played Santa for his growing brood in Portland, establishing a family tradition that continued when the Johnsons moved back to Junction City. "When it first started, my dad's hair was still red," says Becky McAllister, a daughter who teaches now in Portland. "He had a string mop that he used for a beard and he wore an old red coat." Fortune did not always smile on Johnson, and his wife and seven children remember that the family was often poor. But as Santa Claus, he could do no wrong. It was perhaps twenty-five years ago that the tradition moved outside the Johnson home. It flowered in settings like schools and nursing homes and the First Christian Church of Junction City, where Johnson sometimes sang in the choir.

At some point in time, in ways that those who witnessed it still recall with wonderment, it became more than just a holiday amusement. It came to affect, first, the way Johnson looked, then the way he thought. It began, perhaps, when some small child tugged once too often at the nylon beard of the church's old Santa suit, a beard that Johnson already thought was scratchy and uncomfortable. And so he began growing his own, a ritual that starts in May of each year. Suddenly, being Santa Claus was no longer just a Christmas job. Children, perfect strangers, would touch him on the arm in midsummer and say, "Hi, Santa." Others, traipsing in from Laurel Park, just across Kalmia Street from his home, would show up at the door asking for Santa.

A few years ago, Johnson took to repairing toys and keeping a few around the house. The right sort of wistful look, especially on the face of a child from one of the transient families staying at an aging motel down the street, will produce a Christmas gift even in baseball season.

"When I was a little kid, I never in my life had anybody saying, 'I love you,' or giving me a hug," says the man whose life has been reshaped by Christmas. "Now I get hugs all the time. Anytime of the year, I just say to people, 'I need a hug,' and I get one. Maybe I was born a ham. I've always liked to entertain. I like to sing for people. I like to give things away. If you go to making stuff and selling it, you don't get any joy out of it."

Irene Johnson, quiet and methodical, has been Santa's booking agent since things took off. Each year, through the holiday season, she accepts requests for him to appear at large and small gatherings. Much of the work, particularly at nursing homes and schools, is done without charge. Organizations and families that book Santa for appearances customarily provide a few dollars, although he will never quote a fee or ask for payment. Irene is his driver. Many years, he works until midnight on Christmas Eve, dashing to homes where children and adults wait for Santa's arrival.

But that schedule never crimps his own holiday. One of Santa's secrets is that three of his sons are firemen for the city of Portland and two of his daughters are

FAST DOGS AND WHIMSICAL LADIES

married to Portland firemen. So the Johnson clan's big Christmas gathering is always held a few days after the holiday, when Santa Claus and all the firefighters can schedule some time off. Of course, Santa shows up in uniform, fulfilling an annual mission that is defined to the grandchildren as a post-delivery checkup on all the toys that arrived at Christmas.

"He has a way of making children believe that is simply incredible, even when they know him," says McAllister, stepping back and taking a teacher's analytical look at her father's work. "My own kids are old enough to know better. But when he puts on that suit, he is Santa Claus. They make the crossover totally. At that point, he's not their grandfather anymore."

At seventy-three, with health that is less than perfect, Red Johnson is not sure how many years he has left to play the role of Father Christmas. But he is not through yet. There may be some magic in that old red suit that Irene sewed together so many years ago.

"Sometimes I don't know where I get the strength. I'm short of breath and my legs aren't good. But when I'm Santa Claus the strength just seems to come to me. It's so much better to do this and spread some happiness when you can, instead of sitting home feeling sorry for yourself. When I show up in a Santa suit, I never have to ask for love."

Epilogue: Since 1986, Red Johnson has continued his Christmas season work. Christmas of 1988 saw him slowed by poor health, but he still made dozens of appearances during the holiday season.

From mountain vistas to tiny townscapes,
Oregon's land so often seems to shape
the work and play of those who live upon it.

LONELY
GRAVES AND
DESERT
CAFES

The earth is all the home I have
— "The Wandering Jew"
SIR ROBERT AYTOUN

OREGON'S GEOGRAPHY IS WELL-WORDED and well-pictured. Writers, photographers and artists limn the scenery of this corner of earth with new offerings each year. But as a journalist, I write most often about people, seldom about mountains and waterfalls. Still, place seems to be a part of much that I do, if only because so much that the people of Oregon do, in public moments and in private ones, is rooted to the land.

Spectacular landscapes notwithstanding, the Oregon places I am drawn to are places of people. Some are remote and pristine places, but places of special significance because of what people have done there, because of what happens there. A few are almost institutions — a monument standing over the bodies of eight men deep in an Oregon wilderness, an isolated cafe in the vastness of the Eastern Oregon desert.

Some places fascinate because they are such intriguing intersections of humanity and geography. Why would a young, educated couple take their children, along with their hopes and dreams, to settle in a windblown ghost town? Why would an accomplished dance teacher establish her ballet studio in a tiny community's saloon?

And some of my best-remembered places — a police officer's lonely patrol across endless miles of sagebrush, the scene at a portable war memorial that stood for only a few days in Oregon — existed only at the moment people were there.

The commonality of those places is choice. Oregon is abundantly stocked with people who make clear, conscious choices of what they will do. And almost always, it seems, the element of where they will do it is central to the choice. The places they choose tell stories.

High rollers and fast travelers
favor the wide-open reaches of Highway 95,
and reality says that,
in the vastness of the desert,
a lone cop will never catch them all.

Highway 95
Autumn

THE LONGEST BEAT

T HIS IS THE TROPHY TIME OF NIGHT," says Wayne Denney as the patrol car wheels southward through deepening desert twilight. "This is when it's real easy to nail some animal coming out of the brush."

Only minutes later, with the neon of McDermitt, Nevada, in view miles across the flats, a lone coyote streaks through the glare of the headlights. Eastbound on some important bit of coyote business, the four-legged sprinter exits left into the darkness. The road ahead is empty again.

It is big, empty country out here on the long stretch of Highway 95 that slices across the sagebrushed corner of southeastern Oregon, and it makes for the longest, loneliest police beat in Oregon. Those who have done it have stories to tell. Tales of plucking stranded families from winter snowdrifts in one of North America's most sparsely populated regions. Tales of waiting in the dark with the dead and the dying while ambulances and helicopters race across the miles to lonely accident sites. And tales, too, of the double takes an Oregon State Police patrol car can get when it is parked for the night at a motel just across from the Say When Casino in McDermitt.

For the troopers who work the Highway 95 run out of the state police station in Ontario, Oregon, it is a two-day trek. Patrolling the lonely stretch of highway means driving through miles and miles of Idaho and sleeping in Nevada. "I don't have any police powers when I'm over the state line," says Denney. "I'm just a citizen in a police car. But that doesn't mean we'll ignore a dangerous situation just because we're not in Oregon. A few years ago I spotted a guy driving down the road in Idaho and drinking a fifth of whiskey. It took me all the way to Homedale to get him stopped. I just held him until an Idaho officer could get there. I don't think the guy ever knew that he'd been stopped by a patrol car from Oregon."

Elsewhere in Oregon, Denney's state police colleagues typically handle patrol areas that cover twenty to fifty miles of highway. The Highway 95 patrol is two hundred miles one-way. With the backtracking that is a normal part of chasing

---

speeders or working accidents, the run easily can spin out to five hundred miles on the two-day shift. Covering Oregon's lonely lower right-hand corner, an area larger than several Eastern states, has always been a problem for the state police. Around the Ontario office, it is known as the Jordan Valley run, although it ranges more than a hundred miles beyond that tiny Oregon city.

At spots on the route, a lone trooper can be more than an hour away from an ambulance and, in a dangerous situation, even farther from backup help. Officers who work the run regularly do more hands-on first aid than troopers in areas where emergency medical teams are closer. And, in the vast reaches of the desert, they often have to take responsibility for getting stranded motorists to food and shelter.

Before some budget cuts came down a few years ago, the state sent troopers down Highway 95 on five-day stints. But, in recent years, coverage has been scaled back to a weekly two-day patrol of the area. A pair of resident sheriff's deputies assigned to Jordan Valley provides the only other law enforcement presence in the 3,000-square-mile sector of southern Malheur Country. Each of the dozen or so officers working out of Ontario catches the Jordan Valley run several times in the course of a year. At fifty-two, an Eastern Oregon native with eighteen years of patrolling from Ontario behind him, Denney has seen his share of time on Highway 95.

"There are some of us who enjoy doing this run," he says. "And there are a few who are just glad when it's over. I like it. It's a change of pace. It's an area where I've made some friends. It can be pleasant at times like this. But in the winter, when she's full of ice and snow, it's a whole different story."

Isolated though it is, the road carries a fair amount of traffic. It is the pipeline that funnels drivers from Boise, Spokane, and other northern points to the gaming tables of Nevada and the vacation lands of the Southwest. High rollers and fast travelers, too often. The wide open spaces encourage wide open speeds. The thin blue line that patrols Highway 95 does what it can and lives with the vexing reality that it will never catch all the speeders. Enough, instead, to surprise a few, to establish a presence that will give pause to the many and to concentrate on nailing those who drive the fastest.

Radar and a fast Chevy helps. "It's not uncommon at all out here to write speeds in the upper eighties and lower nineties," Denney says. "And once in a while you get a real hummer."

In the most typical drill, the speeder rockets past Denney bound in the opposite direction. The trooper brakes the patrol car to the shoulder, swings the quickest possible U-turn and heads back in pursuit. If the driver is going eighty or more and has not slowed, and if other traffic has slipped between the culprit and the patrol car, then it can take several miles at speeds in excess of one hundred miles per hour to bag the quarry. For those who are surprised to encounter the tall, soft-spoken trooper in an area that seems made for fast driving, it can seem an unfriendly game. But they have not spent anxious hours with Denney at roadside, patching injuries and waiting for the helicopter from Boise or the ambulance from Jordan Valley.

"This road has more than its share of one-vehicle fatal accidents," he says as the speedometer rolls to 115 in a brief chase. "It's isolated, and people get lulled driving on these long straight stretches. Pretty soon high speed doesn't seem fast at all. Then they get into trouble and they find out the laws of physics haven't changed. It still takes a long time to stop a car going that fast."

After the ticket is written, Denney makes some notations in his logbook, smiling ruefully at the driver's explanation that he was searching for something on the floor of his pickup truck at the moment the radar tagged him at eighty-three. Denney has learned to live with the imperfections of a world where the speeders outnumber the cops. "You think a lot about what's fair," he says. "You can only be in one place. You can't stop everyone. Take someone who's going seventy-eight. It's definitely fair that they get a ticket. It's not fair that the other people going just as fast go by while you're writing that ticket and don't get caught. But you can't empty the whole ocean with one bucket."

The patrol car trip down Highway 95 has its pleasant moments. Meal stops at the Old Basque Inn in Jordan Valley and the Burns Junction Cafe in mid-desert are among the best. McDermitt, which is Denney's most frequent overnight stop, does not have quite the same hominess. The turnover at the Say When Casino and restaurant is high. Denney seldom sees the same faces there from one run to the next. Except at the blackjack table, where he ritually spends an off-duty hour out of uniform and sacrifices ten Oregon dollars to Nevada's economy.

"Technically, the overnight time is your own on this run," he says. "You can even have a beer. But one's about it—because you're always on call if there's an accident out on 95. More often than not, you'll get a call." The calls come in many shapes, often relayed across the citizens band radio network by truckers and bus drivers. The regulars who drive Highway 95, especially in the extremes of winter and summer, know that being stranded on the desert has its own perils.

"In the winter, it gets brutally cold out here on the desert," Denney says. "And some of the distances are vast. One of our prime concerns is that someone doesn't get stranded out here and freeze to death. It could happen. There was a case several years back where a guy froze to death up by the Crowley Ranch. And it's not unusual in the summertime to find destitute people stranded out in the middle of the desert. They've started out with a poor vehicle or bad tires, and then they're broken down out there in the heat. A lot of the time, they're in circumstances where you can't just leave them."

Sometimes the needs go beyond calling a tow truck and driving away. On Highway 95, it is common for a trooper to load stranded motorists or uninjured accident survivors into his patrol car and haul them miles to a restaurant or a motel. But, in his own moment of need, the officer often is alone. The isolation of the long run through the desert weighs heavily when the trooper must stop a suspicious car or face a driver who might be combative.

"Out here, where help's so far away, you really have to learn to read the situation when you make a stop. You have to appear relaxed and yet be like a coiled spring, ready to react. If there's any help available, you're going to get it. But sometimes you just have to make the stop alone. It's not trying to be a hero. It's just that you get situations where you don't have a choice. You have to do something. You try to be careful and you use good judgement. There's just not a policy that's ever going to cover every situation that you run into out here."

Epilogue: Wayne Denney still catches his periodic shifts on the long and lonesome Jordan Valley Run.

Years of rain have washed away the ash
and rotted most of the rubber and fabric,
and now wild iris and manzanita
finger their may through torn metal.

Brookings
Spring

A Place of Rest

It is, perhaps, the loneliest and most forgotten cemetery in Oregon.

Four decades ago, eight young American military men died there, deep in a mountain wilderness. Like battlefield casualties, they were buried where they fell. No grieving families stood by, no bugles played, no rifles fired salutes.

Only a sodden and bedraggled little search party of sailors, forest rangers, and Curry County woodsmen were there amid the misshapen wreckage of a twin-engine bomber. In rain and mud and the severest of weather conditions, with the Chetco River running at full flood just below them, the searchers had become a burial detail. Between a shattered wing and the shell of the fuselage, they closed the eight graves, rolled up soggy tents, loaded their packhorses and began the long, uphill trek back to civilization. It was February 13, 1945.

Now, on a spring day, light and shadow dapple a huge monument, an even more unlikely sight in the wilderness than the surrounding wreckage. Years of rain have washed away the ash. The aluminum gleams brightly in the spring sunlight. Wild iris and manzanita finger their way through torn metal. A dogwood tree bows gently forward—a leafy, sheltering hand over the gravesite. The man in the uniform, who comes here more often than anyone, surveys the scene.

"It's still really isolated and really hard to get to," wilderness ranger Rene Casteran says. "I don't imagine ten people a year come in here." In fact, the only predictable visitors at the Navy Monument in the Kalmiopsis Wilderness are Forest Service workers like Casteran.

Military officials decided forty-two years ago against trying to bring out the bodies of the eight men whose patrol bomber went down in the Chetco country in the closing months of World War II. The mountain above the monument drops steeply over two miles of tumbling ridges. The canyonside grade approaches sixty-five percent in some stretches. It plunges from the three thousand-foot mark, where the bomber clipped a tree, to the canyon bottom, where the south fork of the Chetco, barely more than a creek at this elevation, rushes over boulders.

The plane went down January 31 of 1945. Henry Payne, a trapper who had grown up in the Chetco country, was camped three miles away at his lean-to on that cold and foggy day. "He was a man who knew all this country," says his son, Ken. "He worked on trails and did a lot of work back in the woods. In the winters, he trapped because it was the difference between just beans, or beans with bacon."

Sitting out the storm that afternoon, the trapper and a companion heard a laboring aircraft, so close that they involuntarily ducked. It was six days before word of what Payne heard reached the Forest Service, Oregon State Police, and the Coast Guard in Brookings. They immediately connected Payne's information with the report of a Navy plane missing somewhere north of Eureka, California.

The amphibious patrol bomber, newly built in San Diego, had been on a delivery flight to Seattle's Sand Point Naval Air Station. It flew with a crew of five naval aviators. In addition, two extra Navy crewmen were aboard; and an Army lieutenant had caught a "hop" northward and homeward to Vashon Island, Washington. Somewhere north of Arcata, California, the plane hit rough weather, with high winds and rain. It went down at about three in the afternoon, perhaps struck by lightning. The aircraft exploded and burned in the canyon bottom. All eight men died instantly.

The search for the missing plane was launched in a week-long storm that was flooding streams, washing out bridges, and downing telephone lines. Two preliminary expeditions to sites considered the most likely locations of the downed aircraft were fruitless. Attempts at aerial observation and photography were hampered by the weather. One set of aerial photographs of the wreckage showed the extent of the destruction but was impossible to interpret because the photo plane had been operating at very low altitude beneath the clouds.

By February 8, at the urging of Forest Service officials, the Navy began sharing its aerial reconnaissance with local woodsmen. When the trappers, trail builders, and loggers turned their combined experience to the fuzzy photographs and other snippets of information, they were able to establish the crash site on a map. Getting there, they warned, would be no easy matter.

The next day, sailors, forest rangers, and the local experts headed into the wilderness and the weather with a string of packhorses. The rain never let up. En route, the party was resupplied by a Navy dive bomber that dropped C-rations for the men and bales of hay for the horses. The sailors, a world away from their maritime environment, fared poorly. "Raining again," said one radio message from the searchers. "Weather too rough to fly in supplies. River rising again. Food supplies almost exhausted. Some of Navy personnel sick."

By February 11, the group had reached the site. "It was awesome down in that canyon," Vic Anderson, one of the searchers, told a writer in 1972. "Not a sound but rain striking the metal airplane parts."

Part of a day was lost while the commander of the Navy detachment struggled, across the limitations of radio communication, to convince his warm, dry superiors of the ruggedness of the terrain and of the futility of attempting to remove the bodies from the site. Finally came the order to bury the eight men beside the aircraft. Although the burial was completed by February 13, it was not until February 20, almost three weeks after the crash, that all of the searchers and their equipment were out of the forest.

The next summer, a Forest Service crew trekked back to the site and mounded stones over the graves to prevent animal depredation. Eight small wooden crosses were set in place. Soon, the forest began taking back the site.

That might have been the end of the story. But, in 1955, veterans' groups in Curry County began complaining about military neglect of the graves. Oregon congressmen took up the issue, too. In 1957, the Navy agreed to cover all costs of an eight-foot concrete monument and contracted with the Forest Service to provide the work.

The monument, so large that it would be prominent even in an urban cemetery, was a venture that posed almost as many difficulties as the original search. Roy Weideman, a Brookings general contractor, agreed to take on the job. At that time, the crash site was outside the boundaries of the wilderness area, so the Forest Service was able to authorize punching in a rough, four-mile trail with a small bulldozer. Even with that access, the task of moving in over a ton of bagged cement—plus sand, reinforcing steel, an electric cement mixer, and a portable generator—was formidable.

Weideman and a crew of four helpers spent a week living at the site. All the gravel for their concrete mix was carried by hand from the Chetco riverbed below the gravesite. The crew put down a massive slab over the graves, then formed and poured the eight-foot gravestone monolith. Bronze plaques identifying the crash victims were anchored in the concrete. Weideman is eighty-five now, but he has never forgotten the project.

"Everything about that job was hard," he says. "I wanted the finish to be perfect, to look like sandstone. We did the final pour all in one day and I worked until ten o'clock that night down in the canyon, rubbing it out by hand until it was perfect." The monument has two secrets. Deep inside the concrete is a fifty-caliber machine gun that Weideman wrested from the aircraft wreckage. And, out of view on the top of the gravestone, the builder left his initials.

At his home overlooking the ocean near Brookings, Weideman draws satisfaction from knowing that the monument keeps the lives of eight young men from being forgotten. "You know," he says, "the government tried to pay me for that job and I wouldn't let them. It was something I could do for those boys. I never took a dime for that job. It wouldn't have been right."

In 1978, the isolation of the Navy Monument was assured for the indefinite future, when the Kalmiopsis Wilderness was extended to include the headwaters of the Chetco's south fork. The wilderness designation means that the area is legally accessible only on foot. The bulldozer trail is overgrown now, closed in so that it is little more than a path in most spots. It remains dauntingly steep. In the canyon's damp shade, moss grows thickly on the sides and top of the monument. But the face of the stone is kept clear by the hands of occasional visitors, who pluck away the growth when they come to see the memorial in the wilderness.

Epilogue: On September 30, 1987, Homer Ellis of Nevada, Missouri, made a pilgrimage to lay to rest questions that had bothered him for a lifetime. With Rene Casteran as his guide, Ellis, then sixty-one, made the difficult trek to the Navy Monument. Ellis, who was eighteen when his brother, Alvin Ellis, died in the 1945 crash, was the first relative of a crew member ever to visit the site. Roy Weideman, the builder of the monument, died on November 6, 1987.

The man and his machinery
are both outdated,
but Oregon's last steam-powered sawmill
may still be chewing into logs
when the twenty-first century arrives.

Bellfountain
Autumn

Power From the Past

Squint just a bit in the heat. Let the mind's eye close out the electric lights and a few other nonessential modern trappings. Suddenly it is the dawn of the Industrial Revolution.

Overhead the machinery roars and whines in the familiar breezy openness of the sawmill. The big beams—fourteen-by-fourteens today—clatter down the line. But down below, down here where the pilings that support it all roost on the earth, Ralph Hull stands like the engineer of some subterranean locomotive. It is a muggy hundred degrees. Escaping steam susurrates from the fittings, a sable velvet of oil and sawdust coats everything, the twin brass weights of a mechanical governor whirl in the gloom, the great six-foot drive pulley spins on like the balance wheel of some lumber industry time machine. At seventy-four, with a shock of white hair and a mustacheless beard ruffed along his jawline in the style of the Pilgrim fathers, Hull permits himself the smallest smile as he watches the machinery steam machinery—power his lumber company through another day. "The mill's archaic," he says. "And so am I."

Perhaps. But the smart operators, who chuckled for years at an old man and an old mill that had waited too long to modernize, lived to meet the energy crunch and to see the day when electric rates and oil prices climbed faster than a choker setter heading up-canyon at quitting time. Through it all, the only steam-powered sawmill in Oregon huffed on. In the grew-like-Topsy collection of open-sided buildings, a near-perpetual motion machine with moving parts as old as its owner fed sawdust into its ancient boilers to make heat to generate steam to saw more logs to make more sawdust to make more heat . . .

When the smart operators were laying off the help or limping away to bankruptcy court as recession whipsawed Oregon's timber industry in the early 1980s, Ralph Hull's Hull-Oakes Lumber Company kept its boilers fired. Since the steam-powered head rig bit into its first log in 1939, the mill has never had a shutdown or a plantwide layoff. At the mill, which is wedged in a valley of Coast

Range Mountains midway between Corvallis and Eugene, even the lumber is archaic. Big beams, hulking structural timbers of the sort that almost nobody cuts any more, are the company's best-known product. Big, in this case, means up to 110 feet in length and 30 inches in thickness.

In the late twentieth century, construction innovations like prestressed concrete, glue-laminated wood, and factory-built trusses have cut substantially into the old-time market for big timbers. But in many applications there are no suitable substitutes. And, from the docks of Amsterdam to the mine shafts of Cape Town to the shipyards of South America, the Hull-Oakes mill still is known as the provider of the big wood from the forests of Oregon.

In the state's timber circles, its owner has his own reputation. The generation of timber barons and lumber company owners now easing toward retirement knows Hull as a skilled operator who was hardened though not embittered by a series of cataclysmic failures that would have done lesser men. In many ways, the man whose mill runs on outmoded technology looks and talks like he would be more at home in the nineteenth century than in the twentieth. His speech is measured, almost Victorian. Often, he abandons the word, "I," resorting instead to "we" or "us" when speaking of himself.

"In a year, we lost the million dollars and the two mills," he says, as he recounts the most devastating failure of his life. "It was everything we had. We came back to Bellfountain and went to work driving a dump truck. It was good therapy for us. It was good for our health."

Around Monroe, the nearest town of any size, he is known as a quiet, well-read, much-traveled man, a rural patrician who still wears overalls to work, is tight with a dollar, slow to shift to new ideas, and demanding—yet paternal—with his employees. Almost two decades ago he was in the forefront of a group of conservative farmers and businessmen who resisted major expansion of Monroe High School.

But turn the flinty exterior just a bit and other things are reflected. A ping-pong table stands in the back room of the simple frame house that is the Hull-Oakes office building. The paddles and balls wait in the upturned palmate antlers of a huge moose head hanging on the wall. On occasion, Hull has been known to make a visiting salesman go a round across the net, or over a checkerboard, before getting down to business. On the walls of his office are dozens of photographs of medical and religious missionaries in far-off countries. Hull, who supports their work as a personal charity, appears in some of the pictures. He has slept his share of nights in native huts in Africa and South America.

Plenty of people in Monroe remember Hull's stance in the high school expansion battle of the early 1970s and are willing to characterize him as anti-education. But only a handful know that for many years the conservative mill owner subscribed to a string of liberal and progressive publications, which he had sent to the high school library.

"If we hadn't done it, where would those kids have ever gotten exposed to those ideas? We sent them things like Ebony, the black magazine. We hoped that they learned things there that they never could have learned in Monroe. We believe in tolerance and the right of people to be equal. We were making contributions to the NAACP back then, long before it was popular for white people to do that."

"The mill is archaic," says Ralph Hull. "And so am I." But Hull's steam-powered, grew-like-topsy operation has survived, partly because of its old technology, in a marketplace where more modern mills fail regularly. Steam power has brought stability to workers like cutoff sawyer Allen Richter, because the ancient mill has never had a layoff or a shutdown since it opened.

And when it became popular, when the civil rights movement hammered the push for equality into concepts like mandatory busing and employment quotas, concepts that were not exactly what an independent entrepreneur had in hand, Hull bowed out. The man's ideas, like his mill, are uniquely his own.

"There is no place quite like it in the Northwest," says Terry Brown, an Oregon State University specialist in sawmill technology. "A few other mills still have steam running their shotgun log carriage, but nobody is using it to power machinery the way he does. It's the only mill I know of that still has a guy who actually rides on that carriage, setting the rachets on the logs. That's the way they used to do it thirty years ago. You go down to that place and everything there — the steam and the big beams and the old equipment — you can tell it's a labor of love. I don't know of any place that's set up to cut stuff eighty feet long on a regular basis. He's found a niche in the marketplace and you can tell it suits him perfectly."

That sort of stable future hardly would have been predicted for the rough-hewn twenty-two-year-old who decided back in 1934 that he was going into the sawmill business in the teeth of the Great Depression. Signing a contract drafted on the back of a five-dollar check — Hull still has the thumbworn agreement — he leased a shutdown mill. Over the next few years the young man operated several small mills. Two of them, including one in which he had put all of his savings, burned to the ground. When he lost that mill in 1938, he bought the burned-out hulk of another and set about rebuilding it. In the same year, he and his wife, Margaret, were married.

The steampowered operation that he built from the ashes near Bellfountain went into production in the winter of 1939. No electric lines looped into the Bellfountain area then, so every piece of the mill's equipment was powered by steam from the central boiler house. From the first, the mill specialized in long beams, although then, as now, it also cut large quantities of standard dimension lumber. The business grew steadily during World War II and the postwar building boom. Hull plowed much of the profit into timberland purchases. His net worth grew steadily.

In the late 1940s, he began edging out of the operation. He sold the firm to his brother, Homer, but continued to manage it for several years. Then he turned the company over to Homer, took his profits, and headed south to the California redwood country. His million-dollar investment in two redwood mills was lost within a year to a man he describes as a shyster who set up deals designed to fail and used the courts to ensure the result.

"It was hard," Hull says. "In the early 1950s, we came back to Bellfountain and went to work for my brother. We drove a dump truck just to earn enough money to keep going. You don't get over something like that easily. There's something that lingers on. It affects your mental outlook and your confidence in yourself." Nevertheless, he regained enough of that confidence to make a deal for purchase of the mill and timberlands from his brother. In 1955, he and Chester Oakes, the company's logging superintendent, bought the operation as a fifty-fifty partnership. In the mid-1960s, Hull purchased Oakes' half of the business.

"We began to do away with steam in 1955," Hull says. "We had the idea of converting the entire mill to electricity. But when we saw what was happening to our electric bills the process slowed down a little." At present, steam powers the heart of the mill's sawing process, including the bandsaw head rig, edgers, carriage, and log turner. But other equipment, including conveyors, trimsaws, planer, and a new debarker installed a few years ago, operates with electricity. The amount of electrical equipment used at the mill has been essentially stable since 1956. Hull estimates the steam equipment saves $60,000 a year in power bills.

Much of that machinery was manufactured in the early years of this century. Keeping it running is an art in itself. "You do it with a lot of tender loving care," says Ralph Kundert, who is the plant's head millwright. "There aren't many people who can teach you about these machines. When I first came here, I learned by watching the old millwrights. The stuff is very dependable, but taking care of it is a continual process."

Kundert has left Hull-Oakes a time or two for other jobs, but has worked for the company for most of the past forty years. His son, Phil, is the head sawyer. His son, Brad, is a relief millwright and will likely follow his father's footsteps in mill maintenance. He may get to help take the plant's steam equipment into its second century. "I'm not the only guy with sons here," Ralph Kundert says. "There are quite a few. One of our millwrights, Ronnie King . . . his grandfather was working her when the big steam engine was put in."

To the old hands like Kundert, Hull has been known as a hard boss but a fair one. His workers say that he never wavers in the belief that a day's pay should, unfailingly, bring a day's work. But some of the older ones have learned that there is another element in the bargain: more than once Hull has quietly stepped in to help a worker struggling with a financial or personal problem. And there is more: a sort of phantom-of-the-opera dimension that is an open secret between Hull and the crew at his mill.

"He has his way," Kundert says. "For years, we've known that after everybody leaves, he'll be out there walking through the mill. Even when the mill isn't running, he can tell more about how the machinery is going and how the lumber is being cut than most people could if they saw the place operating. He always knows what's going on here."

Epilogue: The Hull-Oakes mill steams on, although it is cutting a bit more standard-sized lumber than in 1986. Its owner is as committed as ever to his antiquated machinery.

It was only a moment in the night
at a memorial for dead soldiers,
but it was captured by a survivor
who came with his music
and the burden of his memories.

Eugene
Autumn

A NIGHT AT THE WALL

"Y OU'LL SEE," SAID EUGENE PSYCHIATRIST *Irwin Noparstak just a few days before the traveling replica of the Vietnam Veterans Memorial arrived. "If it's like it's been other places, there'll be guys standing far away—probably down in the trees by the river—trying to work up the courage to come closer. Some of them won't get there."*

The vet came out of the darkness just before midnight, up from the direction of the river, slogging through mud and a driving rain the way he might have done at Khe Sanh or Hue. He wore a black coat, almost a cape, and the water on it and on his hair glistened in the light of the old street lamps in the park. An orange coal glowed at his mouth and the redolence of marijuana rolled ahead of him like the scent of cordite over a battlefield.

Cradled under his arm was a box, the size of a mechanic's tool case, but worn and leathery, like an old dime store valise. Ahead of him, the raindrops exploded in little bomb bursts on the duckboards spread across the mud. The other vets, the small, clustered knot of them wearing old fatigues and telling old tales beneath the open-sided tent where all the day's the speeches had been made, saw him coming and fell silent.

At the edge of the tent, he rattled the box onto the stage and popped its clasps. He fished inside for a moment, puffing hard, as if the glow from the cigarette could give him light for the task to be done. The clunks and rattles ended. His hands emerged with a bagpipe. He swung the floppy collection of fabric and tubes and fluttering tassels loosely under his arm and strode off quickly to the near end of the floodlit memorial. He squared himself and set off along the length of it, passing panel after panel of names, the unlikeliest and shaggiest and smokiest of generals reviewing the troops.

"It's Mousie," said one of the vets.

"Didn't know if he'd be up to it," said another. "It'll be good for him."

He paused only a moment at the far end, then turned quickly into the darkness behind the memorial. The orange spark disappeared. And the music came.

It floated, in the way that only the sound of the pipes can float. Occasionally, the notes seemed to choke. Then they resumed, higher and keener, the eerie sound of them gliding out of the darkness while little coveys of survivors splashed along the walk out front, their fingers touching the names of men they had known. Behind them, rain hit the spotlights and rolled into luminescent clouds of steam. Cars splashed by on the street above. A man tried futilely to lift a rubbing of a name with a soggy piece of paper.

The vet's one-man Black Watch lasted no more than twenty minutes. He emerged, head down and shoulders shaking, his fingertips trailing against the names on the wall as he marched along its length again. The others watched, too moved to speak, as he came to the tent. The pipes squawked like a duck being shoved into a sack when he compressed them back into the box. He moved off to a tree thirty yards back toward the river, away from the lights and the people. Kneeling in the grass, he stood the long case on its end and rested his hands and head on it. He was there for perhaps half an hour, staring out into the rain. Around one, he was gone.

He never said a word.

In the late hours of the night, when the obligatory dignitaries and the respectfully curious were gone, it was like that at the memorial. The replica evokes the same emotions, taps the same memories, as its archetype. And those who stand more on privacy than ceremony, who remember quietly and grieve the same way, come after midnight.

Even on a chilling night of wind-driven, needling rain they came.

Some who came were couples old enough to be the parents or the grandparents of the dead. And veterans, sometimes with wives carrying umbrellas and standing quietly just a step or two behind them while they searched along the wall for familiar names. Old friends from high school showed up, too. One knelt and prayed in the mud that oozed over the top of the plywood walkway. For some, the darkness, the rain, and the spreading mire in the park matched the occasion and summoned up old mental pictures. "Feels right," said one vet as the mud slopped over the toes of his boots and stirred memories of Southeast Asia's monsoons. "Like coming home."

Those who came to the memorial in the wee hours talked quietly and sparingly. Such assistance as they needed was provided by a handful of reservists and Vietnam veterans. But even the hosting veterans took some time to tend to private business. Standing his shift in the long, wet hours after midnight, Dick Schreiber, a lumber mill foreman from Springfield, lit a small candle beneath one panel of the wall. And remembered.

"Eleven names, all from one day. I was with them. It was at Lai Khe. We were ambushed. We walked into a V.C. base camp. We were pinned down. We had to call in artillery on our own position. We got out and the next day we had to go back and pick up our dead.

"There were about fifty of us in the unit. Some of us still keep in touch. And wherever they take this wall, if one of us lives close, he goes there and lights a candle. It's good. It's helped me."

Floral tributes, ranging all the way from single flowers to giant bouquets, were scattered all along the length of the wall. The designs included a Vietnamese peace symbol and the gold, green, and red campaign ribbon for the Vietnam conflict. But the arrangement that attracted most of the veterans, that drew pensive looks and quiet nods of recognition during the long, wet night, stood alone at the end of the memorial.

Those who took the time to stop and gaze saw a framework of small bamboo branches lashed together, with greenery and tropical flowers rampant around it. Few visitors to the wall except the vets looked closely enough to see the jagged, rusty barbed wire twined through the flowers. But none of them seemed surprised to find it.

"That's Vietnam," said Brian MacDonald, one of the veterans. "That had to be done by someone who'd been over there. The symbolism is all there. It's a beautiful place, just like Oregon. You'd see the little fences that the people would make by tying together bamboo. And there'd be flowers and plants. And in the middle of that beauty there could always be danger—maybe barbed wire, maybe a punji stick. It's like a lot of the other things about that place. You can't understand unless you were there."

Epilogue: Mousie continues to value his privacy, to play the pipes and to live in Eugene, where he runs a small business. Two years after that 1986 night in the rain and the darkness at Skinner Butte Park, I found him and we talked for the first time. "The pipes are how I pray," he said. "I heard four months early that the wall was coming. I knew I would have to do that. I would have to be there. It's the way I scream at God."

When she had scattered his ashes
on the land he had cherished,
she was faced with a choice.
Would she stay to live alone
on the vastness of the desert?

Burns Junction
Autumn

THE WIDOW OF THE OASIS

In summer, the sun rolls up from its bed in the Owyhees, all orange and incandescent, ready to set its feet on the land, to brand the pavement, sear the sagebrush and send jackrabbits to shade. In winter, blitzkrieg storms march from the southwest, jackbooting across the ridges and flats with winds that put tumbleweed in retreat, force cattle to the fencelines, and mount snowdrift battlements across roads.

Big country. And hard, too. Through all of Oregon's history, many have passed across this barren stretch of Malheur County. Only a handful have had the resolve to stay. Appreciation of the desert and its flinty, spare beauty is a gift given only to the few. Weekend visits don't count. Would you live out your life here?

Marge Eckstein would.

"I love the desert. I love the sounds of the desert. I love the view of the desert. I like the changing of the seasons on the desert. The hills become velvet in the spring and then they turn to brown. In the autumn time, the rabbit brush blooms and it's just beautiful."

An unlikely poet, this widow woman who is proprietor of the lonely cafe and gas station that is Burns Junction. Keeper of the only oasis in an area almost the size of Connecticutt. Provider of the rudiments of civilization—plate lunches and unleaded Texaco, telephone and tow truck, coffee for cowhands and directions for strangers. Ninety miles from the desert city of Burns and fifty-five from the Nevada line, Burns Junction is a three-way intersection where Highway 78 meets Highway 95 out in the sagebrush. Open twelve hours a day—or on request when an out-of-gas stranger beats on the door in the wee hours—the junction is a restaurant, service station and small motel.

Electricity arrived on spindly poles barely two decades ago. The United States Postal Service finally instituted local delivery a few years back. And a more or less modern telephone arrived in 1987. Back when Marge Eckstein and her husband, Clarence, bought the place in 1964, the telephone was a hand-cranked model. He had owned a logging outfit and she had done office work before they entered a marriage that was the second for both of them. Their children were grown and gone. The junction had fallen on hard times when they found it. Trucks whizzed by rather than stop and, even though it was the only cafe in several thousand square miles, local families mostly stayed away.

"There was hardly any business at all," she says. "I was open to the challenge of it. I couldn't see any reason why it wouldn't work. There seemed to be enough traffic on the road. But we had a lot of time on our hands after we first took over."

Things changed soon enough. Out on the long, lonesome stretch of 95 that drapes like a ribbon of asphalt crepe over the passes and valleys of southeastern Oregon, truckers yammered on the radio about new ownership at the junction. Closer to home, cowboys, state troopers, ranch wives, game officers, foresters, hunters, desert boondockers, and Reno-bound gamblers began finding their way back. For the new owners it was promising, but strenuous. During that first summer, Marge ran the gas pumps and the kitchen alone. Highway 78 was being rebuilt. Her husband's heavy equipment skills were in demand. The road gang was camped in trailers at the junction. Dinner for thirty, night after night. Easy enough for the daughter of a railroad work gang cook, who had spent summers working in her mother's rolling kitchen out on the Union Pacific mainline. But at the junction, the faces at the table changed often.

"Some of those guys who came out to work on the road didn't stay long," she recalls. "They thought this country was so isolated that they'd been forsaken by God. For them, this was like the dropping-off place at the edge of the world. They'd stay a few days and then they'd be gone."

But even that soon, Marge Eckstein knew that this was home, that she was on for the long haul. She began hiking the desert, learning her way around the vastness that lies between the Owyhee Mountains to the east and the Steens to the west. She came to know the country's flora and fauna, and captured much of it on film. Though she and her husband deprived themselves and worked alone at first, soon enough they were able to hire some help. They built an apartment wing on the restaurant for themselves. Marge moved in a piano and, later, an organ. Through the long desert nights she played classical music and religious hymns.

And, through the twelve-hour workdays, through the blistering summers and the wind-blown winters, she and Clarence became known as the hosts of Burns Junction. He acquired something of a reputation as an irascible desert character, a man quick with a wrench or a quip. In time, the pair became a sort of sagebrush institution, their place a required stop for those who traveled the wide open spaces. But, after a long illness, Clarence died in 1981. And Marge, when she had honored his request to scatter his ashes on the land he cherished, was faced with a choice. Would she stay alone on the desert?

"Losing your mate is losing a living, breathing part of you. I understand that now. I was tempted to leave. But I decided to wait a year. At the end of that year, my son helped me see that I love the place. I knew then that I was going to stay and enjoy it as long as I could."

So she has settled into a routine. Typically, she has a couple living in one of the motel units at the junction, a man to pump gas and drive the tow truck, a woman to help in the restaurant. Bruce and Edith Jacks fill that role now. And Judy Porter comes over from the Flying G Ranch to work a few days each week. Getting live-in help on the desert is sometimes hard. "I don't ever tell my age," says the woman whose home is decorated with pictures of grandchildren. "I lost some help, some people I was trying to hire. They seemed to think that if they came out here I might drop dead on them some day. So now I don't tell."

Life at Burns Junction is comfortable, filled with its own special trials and joys. The elements and the road deliver many of them. Often, when there is tragedy out on the highway, the little restaurant and gas station becomes a command post. Sometimes the injured and the dying are delivered to Marge Eckstein's door. At other times, she is the one who summons distant police officers and ambulances. More than once she has dispatched some of her regular coffee drinkers to do what can be done until help arrives. Sometimes, when the wind is howling and the road is perilous, she goes herself.

"There are nights when it gets slick and icy and it's too dangerous for people to go on. I've had all the motel units full, wall-to-wall people in the restaurant, and strangers sleeping on the furniture in my house. You have to do that. You can't let them go on out there. Some of the accidents you go to are sad, some of them turn out good. I went out on the ice, up on Highway 78 once. Two men. One dead under the steering wheel and the other one like a lost soul. All I could do until the police came was comfort him and try to talk to him. I knew his friend was gone."

In summers, more than two hundred travelers a day come through the door at the junction. Nevada-bound tour buses from Canada stop regularly. The pace slows in winter. When the winds stiffen, the day's visitors can be limited to a frosty state trooper and a few ranch dwellers with cabin fever. The mailboxes for the dozen or so families who live within a twenty-five-mile radius stand in a row just outside the door. Coffee and mail and palaver next to the cafe's wood stove are a seasonal ritual.

Burns Junction is open every day, six to six. But there are plenty of nights when the hours are stretched by a rap on the door for a disabled vehicle or a gas tank on empty. "The ones going to Nevada to get married run out more than anybody else," Marge says. "Stars in the eyes, nothing in the tank."

Her life is full, a life that has long since accommodated to the desert's vast distances. The weekly run to Burns for groceries is a 180-mile round trip. But it takes 260 for the monthly music lesson in Boise. Beyond that, she travels little. Time and the loss of the man who accompanied her to the desert have wrought that change. "The good memories have taken over for me," she says. "I don't need to go anywhere. Now I'm perfectly happy to just stay here day after day among the things I loved and he loved. I'm fortunate. I love people. And I love this place."

Epilogue: Burns Junction is still open seven days a week. Marge Eckstein still answers the night bell when travelers are stranded. She has a new year-round companion living with her at the junction: Marion Haigh, who is ninety and blind, is the retired postmistress of the desert town of Jordan Valley.

In an abandoned town, can
Mark Miller and Linda Donnelly
do any better running floppy disks and
ambitious marketing plans than
others did running sheep and cattle?

Richmond
Autumn

THE GHOST CHASERS

T HE UTTER IMPROBABILITY OF IT ALL comes home only in Mark Miller's second-floor workroom. Next to the flickering screens and keyboards of a bank of computers, the drafty window commands a view of all of Richmond—tumble-down buildings with glassless eyes gazing toward the setting sun, ancient cars moldering back to earth, sagebrush growing where streets once ran.

Looking at the pine clapboards ebbing from burnished gold to dross gray as the light wanes, only the shortest leap of imagination is needed to pull up a vision of some long-ago stagecoach wheeling in from John Day, or homesteaders buck-boarding into town for a Saturday night dance at the Oddfellows Hall. But it is a great leap indeed to come to terms with the idea of Mark Miller and Linda Donnelly buying most of an Eastern Oregon ghost town and moving in with their educations, their aspirations, their children and their budding computer business.

This, after all, is heartbreak country. Across the folded hills, little platoons of poplars that once shaded the homes of hopeful settlers stand in the autumn evening, the yellow-leafed tombstones to dead dreams. For a century, the attrition rate has been high in this arid corner of Wheeler County. Only the strong—perhaps only some of the strong—have survived. Richmond, done in by a set of changes that began with the Great Depression and the improvement of rural roads, died about 1950, when most of its residents had gone and its school had closed.

In this isolated setting, can Miller and Donnelly chase the ghosts from a ghost town? Can they hope to do any better running floppy disks and ambitious market-ing plans than others did running sheep and cattle? "I think we have a real chance to succeed with something nontraditional in this setting," says Mark, who is thirty-five. "We have friends who visit us from Seattle, and they think it's great, but the first thing they want to know is how you make money in a place like this. They don't see how you can afford to be here. Some of it we're still figuring out. But we think it will be possible to make a living right here with our software business. We know the overhead is low. We have quite a few things going already."

Indeed they do. Those oldtime homesteaders who saw winter coming on and knew they still had to build fence, dig a well, roof the barn, and move the herd down to the south pasture would understand perfectly.

"The grand plan," says Linda, pausing in mock ceremony before she plunges into it, "is to rebuild one of the houses. We've already started that. We'd also like to do bed-and-breakfast in at least one of the other buildings. Maybe more than one. And we're talking about restoring the big old business building for the computer operation and for a workshop for Mark. And maybe a little store, too. But we'll keep all the old fallen-down buildings. I don't have any desire to take them down or burn them. They're part of this place."

All of that may sound like the wishful dreaming of some urban refugee with born-again visions of building a new life in rural America. But that is not how it is. Linda Donnelly, who is thirty-one, knows Richmond well. She spent her early childhood there, then came back with her parents year after year, even when every house in town stood vacant. The ground where the town stands was Donnelly land even before there was a Richmond. For her, buying the old town on the road between Mitchell and Spray is her way of latching onto both the heritage of her past and her future.

"My great-grandfather homesteaded this area," she says. "Around 1886, when there got to be enough homesteaders around here that they wanted a church and a school and things like that, he donated the land for this town. They built the church first. My grandfather and my father were born here. I lived here until I was four or five. We were one of the last families in town. My parents sold their part of the ranch and we moved away. But we always kept this old house. We came back every summer and spring break and hunting season, too."

Almost a decade ago, she met Mark Miller, a Seattle native. Soon enough she showed him Richmond. By the time they were married, getting back to Richmond sometime, somehow, was part of their plan. Mark had wrapped up a University of Washington degree in forestry and computer science; Linda had completed three years as an education major at Oregon State College.

In the early years of their marriage, Mark did work for the Forest Service. Linda often assisted on those contracts, which ranged from tree planting to technical forestry projects that enabled Mark to use his computer background. The jobs dictated an itinerant life-style, but in the winters the couple and their growing family often lived in the house that Linda's parents still owned in Richmond. Mark spent the long, cold months working on computer projects.

When they were in Richmond, Miller and Donnelly shared the town with Louis and Pat Bratton, a retired couple who had acquired the old Richmond church and moved a mobile home in beside it in the mid-1970s. The Brattons work to maintain the old church and keep it open for visitors. A minister comes once a year to hold a service there on a summer Sunday, an event that serves as a reunion for old-time Richmond residents.

As years slipped by, Mark Miller's computer expertise began to dominate his working life. Consulting and programming jobs took up more and more of his time. KayuSoft International, the business partnership that he and Linda formed, landed a computer contract with Weyerhaeuser Company in Seattle, did some work for the Oregon State Forestry Department, set up a campaign management

LONELY GRAVES AND DESERT CAFES

program for a Washington State legislator. Other projects, including some original programming work aimed at the consumer market, were keeping the couple in Richmond more and more.

The upshot of all the activity was a decision by the Donnellys to buy most of the town. They did some checking and found that a lumber company had bought most of the abandoned property in the community. The couple persuaded the company to sell, for $15,000, its eight acres in Richmond, including the shell of the town's major business building, several houses in various states of repair and assorted outbuildings.

Now, while they continue to live in the old house owned by Linda's parents, Mark spends every spare moment working on a massive overhaul of the best of the houses on the property they bought. The place is to be a home for the couple and their children, Celeste, Cy, Emma, and Wyatt.

Celeste attends school in Spray, sixteen miles away, and her parents expect that her siblings will follow her there. Mark and Linda look forward to raising their children in Richmond, at least through the elementary school years. The isolation is relieved a bit by the 1947 Stinson airplane that Mark flies from a landing strip at a nearby ranch.

And Linda, to be sure, will teach her children all that she knows about the tiny town and the memories it stirs. "It was never real big," she says. "Maybe twenty houses at the most. A lot of them are gone. But Richmond was a town. People voted here and they had a store and a post office. Before the roads were good, some women and their children used to move to town in the winter so the kids could go to school. I remember it best in the 1960s, when I was a kid. There was one family—the Trents—that had stayed after the school closed. They were here, and that kept the vandals out. So for twelve or fifteeen years it was a perfectly preserved little town that looked like the 1930s.

"In the school, the piano and the desks and the books were all there. We'd go to the school and play school. We'd go to the church and play church. Then the Trents moved away and things started getting stolen and torn up. There were about a dozen years before the Brattons came when nobody lived in Richmond at all."

Mark Miller, the man who married a woman with a town attached, can tell those stories, too. Sometimes, he talks about Richmond as if he were there in its heyday. It is an ideal setting for much of his work. "The kind of software work and consulting I do is a lot like being a writer, because you can do the creative stuff anywhere. As long as I'm able to travel and see my customers when I need to see them, it doesn't make much difference where I am. I'm looking forward to finishing the house so we can start on the big building and get the computer operation moved into it. We're going to get Richmond's business district going again. We call it our urban renewal project."

Epilogue: Since 1986, Mark Miller and Linda Donnelly have created a computer software package that is used by law enforcement agencies to analyze crime scenes. Their satisfied customers range from the FBI to several national police agencies in Europe. Linda has become a midwife and serves the families that live in the sparsely populated region surounding the town. Her parents and her ninety-seven-year-old grandmother have moved to Richmond. Work on the town's structures continues.

The backstage ambience
of a rural saloon's bare brick walls
and the wondrous light
that flows from its towering wall of windows
make it a perfect school.

Oakland
Spring

THE BARRE AT THE BAR

LIGHT CASCADES THROUGH A WALL of glass and tumbles into the vast, high-ceilinged space, playing red-orange games on the bare bricks and ricocheting in a thousand angles off the facing mirrors. Strains of Mills' "Interlude" caress the room as the Regulator clock's pendulum, on time but off beat, clacks away.

The ballerina leaps and spins, satin slippers touching smartly on a floor that gleams with a patina laid down by nearly a century of loggers' boots and farmers' brogans. On she soars, a vision in ivory lace, twirling now past the beer taps and the mahogany back bar, now before a gaggle of mothers roosting at the wood stove, now over the bullet holes in the floor.

So it is behind the towering twelve-foot double doors that a pulpit-thumping Oakland pastor once called "the swinging gates to hell." The Adam's Apple Saloon, known for years as the roughest spot in town, has fallen on genteel times. Satan and John Barleycorn have been routed. In their place stands Francine Quinn, a replacement who is formidable only to the 125 students who show up each week to endure the rigors of dance training. Francine, who began a lifetime of teaching when she was younger than many of her pupils, has former students dancing professionally around the country. And experienced professional performers and instructors show up regularly to give master's lessons at the studio where the barre is bolted to the bar.

"The people of Oakland were very good to us when we opened, but they all said that nobody could ever make a go of a ballet studio in a town this small," Francine says. "I remember that the mayor figured we'd last six months." That was nearly a decade ago, a period in which Francine has seen her art-in-the-boondocks venture blossom. The Oakland Studio of Dance Art, housed in a historic building with a colorful past, is now a solidly established institution on the town's artfully preserved nineteenth-century main street.

The preservation effort, which draws visitors off Interstate 5 and into tiny Oakland, was just beginning when Francine and her husband, Joe, arrived in 1977.

Behind her were years of work as a dance instructor, work that began in Flint, Michigan, only a few years after she took her first dancing lesson.

"I fell in love with dancing," she recalls. "At the age of eleven I was taking lessons and had ten students of my own. They paid me a nickel a lesson. We put posters up around the neighborhood and had a garage recital." Over the years, her training continued, branching out from her teacher in Flint to a top-ranked instructor in Detroit. Her brother, Gene Myers, trained with her. He would later dance at Radio City Music Hall. But Francine was certain that her schooling was not leading her to the stage.

"I have never danced professionally," she says. "I always knew I was going to teach. I was not the most talented student. I'm a logical, analytical person. When we were learning, my brother was just loaded with talent. I was the one who would always do the detailed dance notes so we could practice at home."

By the time she had graduated from high school and married, Francine was running her own dance studio. Even the arrival of two children did not slow her work, which continued over a period of more than twenty-five years, extending through moves to Sault St. Marie, Michigan, and to Spokane, Washington. She became a certified instructor in the Cecchetti method of dance instruction, one of two internationally recognized ballet instruction techniques. In Spokane, she had 150 students and the satisfaction of looking back as former pupils began to mature in years and professional stature. Her ex-students were making appearances with such troupes as the Northwest Theatre Ballet, the Cornish Dance Theatre, San Diego Ballet, and New York Dance Theatre.

She was divorced in Spokane and later married Joe Quinn, whose professional background was in theater and stage productions. They moved to Corvallis, Oregon, in 1970 when he took a position in the theater program at Oregon State University. The classes she opened in Corvallis soon had a large following. The experience was repeated a few years later, when Joe took a theater position at the University of Portland and she launched classes at a school on Sauvie Island.

But the Quinns wanted out of the city. They began seeking a rural setting for her work. In a sense, Francine's inspiration was Marta Becket. A former New York City ballerina who has attracted international attention since she left the bright lights, Becket performs solo in an old Death Valley theater that she and her husband bought and refurbished. In 1977, the Quinns found Oakland. The town, population 850, was in the midst of the historic revival that has put the city's entire downtown area on the National Register of Historic Places.

"We really didn't care how small the town was," Francine says. "We didn't come thinking about a set of numbers or an amount of dollars to earn. We were looking for a life-style and the chance to do things the way we wanted."

The Quinns planned to open in a small downtown building but learned that the saloon, which had been closed for a few years, was available. For both of them, the huge space, with the backstage ambience of its bare brick walls and the wondrous light that flowed from a towering wall of windows, seemed perfect for their venture. The elegant mahogany bar, the old wood stove, and the two bullet holes in the floor—punctuations to some long-ago celebration or altercation—added their own offbeat charm. Joe's talents as designer and set builder bent handily to the task of converting the old saloon to a dance studio.

Work shoes for sylphs, ballet slippers repose on a bench during breaks in classes and are stored in an old, glass-doored beer cooler between sessions at the ballet studio in the Oakland saloon.

Since then, the students have come steadily. In the main, they are from small towns within a forty-mile radius, communities populated by loggers, farmers, and urban commuters who drive off daily to white-collar jobs in places such as Roseburg and Eugene. "It really is just great to work with students from a rural area like this," Francine says. "Sometimes, when you're working in a larger city, you get pupils who've had two or three other instructors. You spend a lot of time reteaching or making them understand how you do things. Sometimes you get resistance. Here, you just have all these kids who are very receptive."

As in most dance schools, only a few pupils will go on to careers in the art. But already a few graduates of the Oakland school appear headed toward work as performers or dance teachers. To others in the field, that would not be surprising.

"What Francine and her husband, both of them, have done to promote ballet in their rural part of the state is wonderful," says Eric Hyrst, director of the State Ballet of Oregon and an internationally recognized performer and choreographer. "She has the kind of dedication you see in people who are putting their whole life into dancing, not just dropping by the wayside after a few years. As a teacher she's very diligent, and her students are always well-trained and well-disciplined."

For Francine, her students' progress, whether it leads to a dancing career or not, is satisfaction enough. "I have taught all my life, ever since I was a teenager," she says. "For me, teaching seems to become more of a challenge every year. This is my life. This is something I'll never change. I can't imagine doing anything else."

Epilogue: Since 1986, Francine and Joe Quinn have separated. The dance school continues under her direction. Often, the parents of dance students help with repairs on the old saloon. The school's graduates have appeared with professional ballet companies in Oregon, Washington, and California.

"If you don't like people,
this is not the place to be.
But I've always figured
that I only have to put up with 'em
for two minutes."

Wheatland
Summer

THE VOYAGER

OFF TO PORT, or perhaps starboard, a heron wades into the shallows for an
evening toe-dip. And across the bow, or maybe the stern, a July sunset pinkens the
feathers of a covey of clouds roosting over the Coast Range Mountains.

Hard to tell left from right, or front from back, on a boat that docks with either
end two hundred times a day. Over and back, over and back. For nearly a century
and a half it has been that way at the Wheatland ferry, a Willamette River crossing
older than the state, a place where illustrious Oregon pioneers such as John
McLoughlin and Jason Lee were once regular passengers. Daniel Matheny, who
stepped off the end of the Oregon Trail to drive his claim stakes near the riverbank
hamlet of Wheatland, fourteen river miles north of Salem, was the man who saw
the unbridged Willamette as opportunity, not obstacle. In 1844, he spiked together
a rude log-and-plank craft that, for a fee, hauled homesteaders, trappers, fortune
hunters, horse traders, missionaries, and early territorial politicians.

At the helm of the *Daniel Matheny IV,* the work goes on for Irvin Hersha. At
fifty-one, he is a third-generation Wheatland ferry skipper. No covered wagons
and no buckskinned travelers these days. But almost everything else—from ten-
speed bicycles to eighteen-wheel trucks—clatters across the steel aprons of what is
now Oregon's largest and busiest public ferry.

"I always figured this was the last place in the world I'd be," says Hersha, who
has spent more than thirty years crossing the Willamette. "I'd grown up around the
ferry and I took off when I got out of high school. I figured that I was going to live
somewhere else and do something different. The first thing I knew, I'd moved back
and had a house next to my Dad. The next thing I got was his job. He had a heart
attack on the ferry one Sunday. I was twenty-one, and they asked me to fill in. I
never got away from it."

Hersha's command, the *Daniel Matheny IV,* displaces forty-nine tons and is
powered by electricity. Operated by the government of Marion County, the vessel
runs sixteen hours a day on a year-round schedule, with occasional interruptions

for high water or mechanical problems. Smaller craft that cross the Willamette at Buena Vista and Canby are Oregon's only other public ferries. Just a half-century ago there were scores like them around the state, including one at every coastal town where a river met the Pacific. The Wheatland ferry, which moves more than one hundred fifty thousand cars and trucks in a typical year, is the only crossing in a thirty-six-mile river stretch between bridges at Salem and Newberg.

After Daniel Matheny's original vessel made its last crossing more than a century ago, Wheatland was served by a series of ferry operators who ran small, home-built wooden vessels. Most of those early ferries were large enough to carry only a single wagon and horse team. They ran on a fixed line strung above the river and were powered by horse teams on shore. Hersha's grandfather, whose forebears came to the northern Willamette Valley in 1852, worked on one of those vessels during the early part of this century. Marion County took over the ferry in 1934, eliminating fares and putting the name *Daniel Matheny II* on the gasoline-powered vessel in use at the time. The *Daniel Matheny III,* powered by electric motors, was launched in 1944.

The current boat, Wheatland's first steel ferry, took to the water in 1959. It can complete a round trip, including loading and unloading on both sides of the river, in about five minutes. Without rudder or keel, it is stabilized by huge pulley wheels that run on a cable strung high above the river. The cable parallels a set of electric wires which feed the vessel's twin motors through shuttles similar to those used by urban streetcars. The ferry has no real steering system of its own; the cable guides it across the river.

The *Daniel Matheny IV* serves a productive agricultural area that includes such small towns as Brooks and Amity. In the summer, its vehicle count is doubled by farm trucks, migrant workers, and shunpiking tourists. Loads of corn bound for nearby canneries and hops headed for faraway breweries regularly move across the river aboard the ferry.

"The biggest day we ever had was back in the '70s, in the gas crunch," Hersha says. "Gas went up to about $1.35 and people were looking for any shortcut they could find. One summer night along in there, I knew I was real close to hitting a thousand cars for the day. I kept her open for a few extra minutes that night and got my thousandth car."

The ferry was still free in those days. But that pleasant state of affairs ended in 1981, when a modest fee schedule centered on a fifty-cent charge for cars was imposed. Ferry usage dropped by almost a third. Since then, there has never been a thousand-car day, although Hersha still has the occasional summer day that tops eight hundred. He and two other ferry operators work solo during the winter months but are assisted by on-deck toll takers for the peak crossing hours in the summer season.

In a typical Oregon winter, high water will dock the *Daniel Matheny IV* for thirty or more days. The mooring lines go out when the measured level of the Willamette at Wheatland tops sixteen feet.

Early on a winter day in 1984, the river was approaching that mark when Hersha came to work, expecting to put in a few hours and then shut down the operation. At the change of shift, he was making a crossing with two cars, seven passengers, and Roy Sloan, a new ferry operator, on board. They were well away from the bank when the flood current snapped the overhead guide cable and ripped away the electrical connection. The rudderless, powerless ferry went careening down river. Hersha put out a quick call for help on a battery-powered radio. Then he and Sloan hustled the frightened passengers, including several small children, into lifejackets.

Although Sloan was certain the effort would come to grief, Hersha launched the ferry's twelve-foot motorboat. "We were all going down the river together," Hersha says. "The rest of them were still on the ferry. I got that little boat going and started pushing against the side. Eventually, I got her pushed over to where she was hitting the bank. After about the third bounce, my partner got a rope around a tree and we stopped her. I don't think we were ever in any real danger, but if we hadn't had the little boat, it's hard telling how far we might have gone."

Getting the ferry back to its customary spot and moving passengers and cars onto shore after the unscheduled excursion required the services of two sheriff's departments, several rescue boats, and a tug. But such excitement is rare around the ferry landing. The ferryman's life is largely routine, although at Wheatland in midsummer it can be a hectic routine that offers few pauses. On either bank, there is almost always a car waiting to make the crossing when the *Daniel Matheny IV* noses to shore.

"If you don't like people, this is not the place to be," Hersha says. "But I've always figured that I only have to put up with 'em for two minutes and then they're off of her. In all these years, I haven't met anyone I can't stand for two minutes."

Epilogue: Since the summer of 1987, Irvin Hersha has crossed the Willamette more than thirty-five thousand times.

An untimely death on the desert
left her with a town, her grief,
her precious memories
of her grandfather, and a future
clouded with uncertainty.

Millican
Spring

THE HEIRESS

SHE DID NOT PLAN for it to end this way. Not with the old man's murder. Not with the funeral and the sadness and the devastation of it all. Not with owning a town and pondering its destiny.

A lot to manage when it is just you. Three months back, you were in the home stretch of your college education, with fresh memories of your last trip from California to the old man's lonely, weather-worn outpost on the desert. Just a couple of terms and a European adventure stand between you and graduation.

But now, old Bill Mellin's will says it is yours, this lonely windswept place in cowboy country. And you are only twenty-two and and what will happen to your dream of the Sorbonne in Paris? Hard to ponder, when you are elbow-deep in grease on the old rocking-horse pump that tugs the water up from eight hundred feet below the desert. So, do you hold the town's future? Or does it hold yours?

"I take it a day at a time," Valerie Cornford says. "If I'm meant to leave here and go on to the Sorbonne and do all those things, then it will sell. And if I'm not, if it doesn't sell, then I'll stay. I could stay and be happy, if it came to that."

Riley, Hampton, Brothers . . . and then Millican. Sunbaked, windburned little townlets, hung like so many beads on the long, lonely asphalt reach of Highway 20 that stretches westward through the Oregon sagebrush from Burns to Bend. No accident that they are spaced apart by distances that once would have been a day's wagon ride. Outposts of civilization, then and now, as welcome a sight through the windshield as they were over the ears of a horse team.

The horse teams, of course, always stopped. But the cars mostly sweep by, cruising on the fast side of seventy, their drivers content with the knowledge that gasoline and sandwiches are there for the stopping. Year in and year out, just enough of them stop to keep the remote little cafes and gas stations in business. In the desert string of gas-pump oases along Highway 20, Millican was perhaps the most famous. Robert Ripley, of believe-it-or-not fame, told the nation about the "one-man town" a couple of times before World War II.

The man then was Billy Rahn, who found his way to the desert from Chicago. But decades before him it had been George Millican, who put his name on the trading post twenty-six miles beyond Bend. Millican has gone through a series of hands in its eighty-odd years. The hands of Bill Mellin, Valerie Cornford's grandfather, arrived in 1946. A Navy veteran, he had planned to be a deep sea diver. But in California he stole another man's wife—her name was Helen—and headed off to the Oregon desert with her.

Bill and Helen Mellin bought Millican and never left. Billy and Tina—Tina, who would become Valerie's mother—were born there. It was a good life, if not a wealthy one. Over the years, the Mellins added rooms for the children, a service garage, a tiny cafe, and a two-room motel. Some of the old pine buildings that had been the original Millican were skidded off into the sagebrush. In time, Bill Mellin became a character of the country east of the Cascades, a bit of walking folklore.

"It was him, not the town," says Ed Park, who was Mellin's nearest neighbor at the end. "He was an institution. What was the big deal about Millican? It was just some old buildings, desert artifacts, old junk that desert rats always collect. But Millican wasn't the store. It wasn't the town. It was Bill."

Friendly is not the first word that springs to the lips of those who describe Mellin, although he was that and more to his desert neighbors. For travelers, he was respectful, even pleasant, but quick-tempered with those who criticized the desert or the prices of a tiny, remote business.

His neighbors tell of the tourist who made it to Millican with his fuel gauge fluttering on empty. Mellin came to the pump as the man spotted the prices and muttered under his breath. When the driver asked for just enough gasoline to get to Bend, Mellin paused and looked out over miles of sagebrushed emptiness. "Guess you can get it across the street," he said with finality. He hung up the nozzle and walked back into the store.

Mellin's children moved away when they grew up. Tina married Richard Cornford, a family friend, and Valerie was born. Then life soured for Bill Mellin. Tina was killed in a traffic accident in 1971, when Valerie was five. Mellin's wife, Helen, died in 1976. His son was killed in an airplane crash in 1980. As his immediate family disappeared, Mellin's granddaughter became a central figure in his life.

"Every summer, until I was sixteen, I came up from California and went to the desert to be with him," Valerie says. "June to September every year. I loved it. In the summers, I'd run the store when he was busy. I played in the desert. Grandpa and I would go fishing and camping. He was the only connection I had with my mother. He never wrote letters. But I wrote him three or four times every month. I always told him everything I was doing."

Even after she graduated from high school and entered California State University at Northridge as a business major, Valerie visited the desert. As her grandfather's years advanced, he shut down the garage, motel, and cafe, but continued to operate the store and the gas pumps. He frequently had the town on the market, although the asking price was always aimed for a starry-eyed buyer. None came, so Millican went on, with Bill Mellin as its only permanent resident.

In the fall of 1987, he fell ill. Cornford withdrew from school to spend two months with him. She had the neighbors in for his seventieth birthday party. Then,

LONELY GRAVES AND DESERT CAFES

when he was well enough, she returned to school to wrap up her education and to plan a term of study in Paris. "I never saw him happier than when she was up here that last winter," Park says. "He just glowed."

On a March night in 1988, Mellin was shot and killed. David Wareham, a drifter who had worked for him, was arrested and charged with his murder.

Cornford, her father, and her stepmother came from California for the funeral and a wake, where rugged old ranchers wept and told Bill Mellin stories. When the will was read, Valerie Cornford was the heir to all of Millican.

The town was shut down for two months. But friends of Mellin stepped in to watch the place and to help his granddaughter. Valerie moved into the old man's living quarters at the rear of the store. The bedroom that was once her mother's became her own. She put the town on the market and plunged into weeks of remodeling and painting work. Neighbors pitched in to help and stood beside her as she auctioned off tons of the junk that her grandfather had accumulated. Many of the choice pieces went to local ranchers, who admitted they were buying memories of a friend.

Myer Avodovech, a Bend attorney, assists Valerie in sorting out Millican's future. Like the neighbors who come to swing hammers and paintbrushes at the store, he is amazed by the determination of the town's young heir. "She has a lot of inner strength," he says. "I've watched her go through this process, and it's been very interesting. I see her grandfather in her. She decides very quickly who she's going to like and trust." Avodovech thinks that eventually Millican will sell. His client is prepared for any possibility.

"I've given Millican a facelift," she says. "I didn't want anybody to come here and try to live on my grandfather's legend because they won't be able to live up to it. It's ready for a new owner. I'll stay here as long as I need to. But when it sells, I'm going to be really sad. And I won't come back for a long time."

Epilogue: On June 15, 1988, Millican was sold to Douglas Becker, who now operates the town. David Wareham has been sentenced to life in prison. Valerie Cornford is at the Sorbonne.

ABOUT THE AUTHOR AND PHOTOGRAPHERS

MIKE THOELE was born in Illinois in 1941 and is a graduate of St. Joseph's College in Rensselaer, Indiana. He came to Oregon at twenty-seven, after working on daily newspapers in Indiana. In a twenty-year newspaper career with *The Register-Guard* in Eugene, he has held a variety of writing and editing positions. For more than a dozen years he worked, by choice, in coverage of rural Willamette Valley communities. During a stint as *The Register-Guard's* city editor, he created the newspaper's roving reporter position, which he has held since 1985. He is a part-time faculty member at the University of Oregon's School of Journalism and has served as adviser to the inmate newspaper at the Oregon State Penitentiary. He lives in a log and stone house that he and his family built in the Coast Range Mountains, near the small community of Cheshire.

PAUL CARTER, a Washington, D.C., native and a graduate of the University of Maryland, has been a *Register-Guard* photographer since 1984. He worked earlier at newspapers in Annapolis, Maryland; Logan, Utah; and Missoula, Montana. He photographed the chapters entitled "The Keeper of the Music," "A Matter of Choice," "Doctor Garden," and "Power From the Past."

CARL DAVAZ, *The Register-Guard's* director of graphics, began his career in Kansas as a photographer at *The Topeka Capital-Journal.* He came to Oregon in 1986 from Missoula, Montana, where as the *Missoulian's* director of photography, he photographed and designed the book, *Montana Wilderness: Discovering the Heritage.* In addition to designing *Footprints Across Oregon,* he photographed the stories entitled "The Builder of Better Bugs," "The Traditionalist," "An Oregon Aborigine," "The Man Who Crossed Over," "The Way It Used to Be," and "The Ghost Chasers."

PAT DAVISON, a photography intern at *The Register-Guard* during 1987, is a native of Ohio. He is now a staff photographer at *The Albuquerque Tribune* in New Mexico. Davison, a graduate of the University of Missouri, produced the photographs for "The Hardest Work There Is," "The Old Man of the Bay," and "A Place of Rest."

WAYNE EASTBURN, an Oregon native, arrived in newspaper work with background as a motion picture projectionist and a hobby photographer. He has been a *Register-Guard* photographer for twenty-five years. He photographed the chapter entitled "The Voyager."

GEORGE MILLENER, *The Register-Guard's* assistant director of graphics, came to Eugene in 1984 after working at *The Palm Beach Post* in Florida. Earlier he had worked at *The Des Moines Register.* A graduate of the University of Kansas, he did internships in Lawrence, Kansas; Wichita, Kansas; and West Palm Beach, Florida. His photographs appear with the stories, "Loggin' Man," "The Birdman of Bandon," "The Warrior's Quest," and "Realized Dreams."

ANDY NELSON, a Kansas native, has been a photographer at *The Register-Guard* since May 1988. A Kansas State University graduate, he worked previously at *The Kansas City Times* and served photography internships at *The Kansas City Star, The Denver Post, The Seattle Times,* and *The Philadelphia Inquirer.* He took the photographs for the chapters, "Marathon Men," "The Artisan," "Sawdust and Music," and "The Heiress."

ROSANNE OLSON, a native of North Dakota, is a Seattle free-lance photographer who does editorial, fashion and advertising photography for major United States magazines. A graduate of Minot State University, she holds a master's degree in journalism from the University of Oregon. She worked as a part-time photographer at *The Register-Guard* from 1982 to 1986. Olson's photographs appear with the chapters entitled, "The Evans Creek Flier" and "The Barre at the Bar."

CHRIS PIETSCH has been a photographer at *The Register-Guard* since May 1988. A native of Sandpoint, Idaho, he is a graduate of the University of Idaho. As a student, he did internships at newspapers in Moscow, Idaho, and Spokane, Washington. He later worked fulltime at the *Idahonian* in Moscow, Idaho, and at *The Tribune* in Lewiston, Idaho. He photographed the chapter, "The Mongolian Cowboy."

DAN ROOT, a graduate of Oregon State University, was a *Register-Guard* photographer from 1986 to 1988. Earlier, he worked four years at the daily *Missoulian* in Missoula, Montana. A native of Los Angeles, he is now a graduate student in business at the University of Oregon. Root photographed the chapters entitled "The Thinking Man's Rambo," "From Russia, With Faith," "The Old Man of the River," "The Speed Merchant," "The Historian," "The Real Santa Claus," "The Longest Beat," "A Night at the Wall," and "The Widow of the Oasis."

JOE WILKINS III, a Colorado native, served an internship at *The Register-Guard* in 1988. Earlier he was an intern at the White House Photo Office. A 1989 graduate of the William Allen White School of Journalism at the University of Kansas, he is working as a free-lance photographer. He photographed the chapter, "One More Time."

INDEX